Secrets of Happy Couples

Advance Praise for *Secrets of Happy Couples*

"This book opens doors to places we all want to go, but to where so few of us actually arrive. An inspiring, yet down to earth review of the key components of relationship satisfaction."—Carleen Glasser, co-author of *Eight Lessons for a Happier Marriage and Getting Together and Staying Together*

"No truly satisfying relationship can develop without each person bringing their fullest selves to the dance. Olver unflinchingly depicts what you need to make that happen. Beyond idyllic couples in love, Olver depicts the nitty-gritty choices and mindsets of successful couples. Her sections on deciding to NOT be part of a couple are worth the cost of the book alone."—Paul & Layne Cutright, authors of the bestselling *You're Never Upset for the Reason You Think and Straight from the Heart*

"If there ever was such a thing as a 'relationship training manual,' this is it. This book is a 'must-read' for all single and coupled men and women everywhere who desire a deeply connected and joyous loving relationship. Not only does Olver present real research on what actually works in relationships from the 100 happy couples she surveyed, but she writes in a compassionate, clear and engaging style. Once you start reading this book, you won't want to put it down!"—Dr. Karen Kan, author of *Creating Your Fairytale Love Life: Harness the Law of Attraction to Manifest Your Dream Partner*

"Kim's book shows real insight into the challenges many couples face and she provides a fresh approach in how to respond effectively to these problems. I have already found some of her ideas valuable as a counselor and can highly recommend this book for both couples and counsellors."—Sandra Haynes, counselor and member of the Counselling Association of South Australia

"Kim Olver has written a delightful book on relationships. She shows a fresh take on relationships and problems. She applies a new rule borrowed from business about abandoning the Golden Rule and instead applying the Platinum Rule: Treat people the way that they want to be treated. If we could just incorporate the Platinum Rule in our relationships, conflicts would disappear.

Kim wisely counsels couples to really get to know one another and further to spend time in introspection and get help for past mistakes made in previous relationships before entering new ones. I recommend it highly for good relationships and even more for relationships having struggles."—John Wilder, marriage, relationship and sexual coach

"Kim writes in an easy to read, conversational tone that I found quite engaging, as if she were speaking just to me. I have been an avid fan of Dr. William Glasser's *Choice Theory*, having taught it to my clients for many years, and I was thrilled with the way Kim expanded upon the Destructive and Caring Relationship Habits.

This is a book that the reader can open to any page and find a gem there. I would definitely recommend *Secrets of Happy Couples* to my clients and to anyone who wants to create a successful and happy relationship."—Michelle E. Vásquez, MS, LPC, Relationship Coach

"Jam-packed with ideas, tips and strategies to improve and maintain the love of your life. Anyone who wants to develop and maintain loving relationships needs to read this book."—Dr. Nancy S. Buck, author of *Peaceful Parenting* and *Why Do Kids Act That Way?*

"Secrets of Happy Couples does a great job of summarizing everything that I've ever read on relationships—and in addition includes Olver's unique insights. I keep thinking, as I'm reading, Wow! When I'm in a relationship I'll want to go over this chapter with my partner."—Despina Gurlides, author of *Not a Guru: One Woman's Spiritual Journey to Happiness.*

"I found this book to be a refreshing look at the elements of successful couples through the eyes of the couples themselves. The variety of stories and first hand examples provided the personal touch that made it especially appealing to me. I think readers will be able to see themselves and find room for improvement regardless of the type relationship they are in."—Marcus Gentry, author of *101 Ponderables*

"*Secrets of Happy Couples* is rich with information for how to take responsibility for your own happiness and the happiness you derive from your relationship. The combination of Kim Olver's vast experience and the real life couples she interviewed gives the reader practical advice on relationship subjects you may not have considered before. The extra good news is that whether you are currently in a relationship or single, this book answers the hearts' questions in such a way that your current or next relationship will benefit!"—Sarah Elizabeth Malinak, co-author of *Getting Back to Love: When the Pushing and Pulling Threaten to Tear You Apart*

"Kim Olver put together a great resource utilizing the expertise of some of the top relationship experts to help you attract and keep a healthy relationship. The most important element is that happy relationships start with you and she takes you through the process of discovering the key inside to transforming your relationship experience."—Debra Berndt, America's Love Expert and author of *LET LOVE IN: Open Your Heart & Mind to Attract Your Ideal Partner*

"Secrets of Happy Couples provides a complete guide to relationships, starting before you are in one, taking you through the getting together, compatibility and maintenance stages while ending with how to manage the grief of a relationship ending, whether it be through death, divorce or a personal decision to separate. It's brilliant. Olver provides a road map for success at any stage."—Gina Mollicone-Long, International best-selling author of *Think or Sink*

"Kim's book is very user friendly, an easy to read guide for singles and couples to learn the ins and outs of having a successful and satisfying relationship. She takes leading experts' philosophies and put's them into an easy to understand language for everyday couples."—Dana Vince, Licensed Mental Health Counselor

"Kim Olver, in her book *Secrets of Happy Couples,* brings a hopeful perspective as one experiences the loss of a loved one, through death, divorce or a break-up. She takes the reader into a journey of empowerment as she suggests we have choices in how we respond to the loss. In life, we may experience a loss of a loved one that we may not understand or that leaves us in total despair. It is when we experience grief. Although this is a normal and necessary process, Kim reminds us that we still have choices, and these are: Leave It, Change It or Accept It. Kim makes us aware, above all, that despite any loss, we are capable of finding new possibilities in our lives."—Ligia M. Houben, MA, CG-C, CPC

"As a therapist in private practice for the last twenty, I keep an updated reading list to be able to give to my clients. *Secrets of Happy Couples* is a great handbook for both individuals and couples, clearly written and with practical tools and personal stories that make it engaging to read. I have definitely added to my suggested reading list and recommend it highly."—Joanne G. Weiss LCSW, M.Div., M.A., D.Arts, psychotherapist in private practice, Clarks Summit, PA

"Relationships significantly influence our inner peace and happiness. That's why Kim's book, *Secrets of Happy Couples,* should be required reading for singles and couples alike. This book is one of the most comprehensive coaching resources on sustaining a truly fulfilling and long-lasting relationship."—Mary Allen, author of *The Power of Inner Choice* and *America's Inner Peace Coach*

"Kim has written an outstanding book. As a relationship specialist I am always on the lookout for the best resources for my clients and customers. Kim Olver is now on my 5 Star A List! *Secrets of Happy Couples* is a Godsend for the masses . . . keep it coming, Kim!!"—Ken Donaldson, author of *Marry YourSelf First!® Say "I Do" to a Life of Passion, Power, Purpose and Prosperity*

"It's true, what you focus your attention on grows. In *Secrets of Happy Couples,* Kim Olver does a superb job of helping you identify the most important things to focus on if you want to create and maintain a happy, healthy relationship. We especially enjoyed how she clearly organizes her practical advice into a step-by-step plan for success as a couple. She succeeds admirably at making sure you ask the important questions before and during the relationship, and even more importantly, helping you come up with authentic answers along the way."—Beth Banning and Neill Gibson, developers of The Art of Conscious Connection seminars and authors of the forthcoming book, The Power of WE!

"*Secrets of Happy Couples* has all we need to know about having successful intimate relationships. Simple, down to earth information will help any couple improve their lives. Kim possesses obvious deep insight into human nature that we can all benefit from. One could continue to find value in this book in all stages of life."—Krisanna Jeffery, author of *The Great Sex For Life Toolkit*

"*Secrets of Happy Couples* is a delightful and powerful new book and a must read for anyone wanting to improve the relationship with their partner or spouse. It will prove to be a necessary tool for us, who as therapists, work to help our clients create happier relationships. This is a book I will recommend to all my clients."—Don Childers, LCSW, LMHC, Private Practice, Indianapolis, In.

"A very insightful, comprehensive and uplifting guide. Highly recommended. Ms. Olver addresses all the most pressing issues of couples today"—Dr. LeslieBeth Wish, Ed.D., columnist, Relationship Realities

"I wanted to say thank you for writing this book. I read the whole thing cover to cover over the weekend. I can honestly say it was an educational process and I learned a lot. This has helped me understand things that I didn't before. I just wanted to let you know that this book has changed my life in a very positive way and regardless of the outcome of my relationship, this book has had a great impact on my life."—Alex Kuperman—IT Technician

Book Two of the InsideOut Empowerment™ Series

Secrets of
Happy Couples

LOVING YOURSELF, YOUR PARTNER, AND YOUR LIFE

KIM OLVER

InsideOut Press

Chicago, Illinois

Second in the InsideOut Empowerment™ Series
Published by InsideOut Press
www.KimOlver.com

Cover design: Dunn+Associates, www.dunn-design.com
Interior design: Dorie McClelland, Spring Book Design

ISBN: 13 9780982754900
First edition.
Printed in the United States of America

Library of Congress Cataloging-in-Publication Data

Olver, Kim, 1960-
Secrets of happy couples : loving yourself, your partner, and your life /
[Kim Olver].
    p. cm. -- (InsideOut empowerment series ; bk. 2)
Includes index.
ISBN 978-0-9827549-0-0 (pbk.) -- ISBN 978-0-9827549-1-7 (elec-
tronic book text)
1. Couples--Psychology. 2. Interpersonal relations. I. Title.
HQ801.O48 2011
646.7'8--dc22
                        2010024023

This book is dedicated to those who want more love in their lives.
It's not a mystery any longer.

And to Marcus, the special man in my life,
who teaches me everyday how to be a better person.
Life together just keeps getting better and better.

Contents

Acknowledgments

This book is the result of great collaboration. Many wonderful people generously offered their time, passion, and expertise to create *Secrets of Happy Couples*.

First, Marcus—the special man in my life with whom I share a true InsideOut Empowerment relationship. You teach me everyday about myself, about love, and about life. You support me unconditionally, always encourage me, and consistently challenge me to reach beyond where I think I can go. I love you.

My two sons, Dave and Kyle. Without your support, respect, and love, I wouldn't have finished this book. You may not know it but you are the reasons I want to play big in the world.

My father, Carl Daub, for giving me an early childhood message that I could do or be anything I wanted. I actually believed you. And my mother, Nancy Hankins, for always being the one constant in my life. And my wonderful brothers, Randy and David, whose support I really appreciate.

Denise Daub, my administrative assistant. This title doesn't even begin to describe all you do for me. I am a dreamer and "big picture" person. Without your constant attention to detail, much would be lost. And let's not forget your incredible creativity. You even found the perfect photo for the cover of this book. You are truly my business partner in every sense of the word. I honestly don't know what I would do without you.

Dr. William Glasser, my mentor and the founder of Choice Theory, and all his wonderful instructors who greatly influenced my thinking, personal growth, and development. There are so many: Nancy Buck, Al Katz, Ellen Gélinas, Kathy Curtiss, Stephen English, Linda Harshman, Bob Sullo, Dave Betz, Pat Robey, Tom Smith, Marty Price, Jon Erwin, Sylvester Baugh, and others. You know who you are.

The over 200 respondents to my survey, who are in happy, satisfied partnerships. Without you I couldn't have written *Secrets of Happy Couples*. Without your willingness to take an online survey and discuss intimate areas of your lives, I would not have been able to gain the insights necessary to write this book.

Prominent relationship experts who assisted with the content of the book through their interviews with me: Dr. Gary Chapman, Arielle Ford, Dr. Harville Hendrix, Drs. Gay and Kathlyn Hendricks and Dr. Karen Kan. These great authors and practitioners gave generously of both their time and their expertise to make this a better book for you. For that, I am very grateful.

The many relationship and Choice Theory experts who helped with this book—some I knew, others were strangers. Each of them reviewed at least one chapter of *Secrets of Happy Couples* and brought their considerable expertise to bear in order to make the chapter even better. In alphabetical order, they are: Sylvester Baugh, Beth Banning, Nancy Buck, Don Childers, Lissa Coffey, Jill Crosby, Denise Daub, Ken Donaldson, Marcus Gentry, Neill Gibson, Carleen Glasser, Melody Glatz, Rodney and Karen Grubbs, Sandra Haynes, Ligia Houben, Krisanna Jeffery, Sarah Elizabeth Malinak, Sarah Michaels, Dennis Neder, Rinatta Paries, Margaret Paul, Patricia A. Robey, Betsy Sansby, Poon Meng Seng, Steve Toth, Dana Vince, Neil Ward and John Wilder. You were willing to wade through unedited material which showcases your patience, generosity, and willingness to bring your gifts to the world. I thank you all from the bottom of my heart.

Milli Fitzgerald, a woman I have never met but who so graciously agreed to allow me to use her poem in the Maintenance chapter of *Secrets of Happy Couples*. You embody the idea of maintaining a long-term, committed relationship.

Dr. Tony Alessandra for allowing me to introduce his business concept of the Platinum Rule into the area of couples' relationships.

Terri Winfree, a great friend. You offered to share your timeshare in Cabo with me that first week in January so I could have a beautiful, serene background for writing *Secrets of Happy Couples*. Your generosity is unsurpassed and I will always be grateful. And let's not forget our other two traveling companions, Sharon Case and Libby Khan.

Mr. and Mrs. James and Ora Gentry, married 59 years, who provide a shining example of what it is for two people to be happy and in a long-term, committed relationship. Not only do you love each other, you actually *like* each other and still enjoy deep conversation. Thank you for your kindness and support.

Despina Gurlides, the best editor in the world. Not only did you work your magic by making this book great, but you did it a week ahead of schedule! Thank you.

Kathi Dunn and Hobie Hobart at Dunn & Associates, Strategic Design and Branding for Authors and Experts, for your patience, understanding, and creativity. You designed the perfect cover for this book and did it in half your normal time to meet my deadline.

Dorie McClelland, the best interior designer in the business. You made everything perfect!

Graham Van Dixhorn of Write to Your Market, a true word wizard with the English language. Thanks for sharing your gift with me and *Secrets of Happy Couples*.

Asha Moon, Anne Roach, Karen O'Donnell, Sandra Brown, Pam Thomas, and Peter Zanol for all you do to support me and for helping me reach more people with my survey. And Peter, thank you for connecting me with Sandy.

Reginald Terrell for giving me the idea that all relationships end. How true that is! Thank you.

And last but not least to all the other people who support me. There are too many to mention. That may be my next book. I couldn't keep going day after day without you. Every one of you has taught me the lessons of this book. You have shared your stories with me and helped me better understand love. Thank you, my friends. I love you all.

Secrets of Happy Couples

Introduction

InsideOut Empowerment

You can't change the direction of the wind,
but you can adjust your sails.

—Jimmy Dean

Having successful interpersonal relationships is of the utmost importance in life. When we get along well with the important people in our life, everything else seems to fall into place. Even those things that we deem challenging do not seem as difficult, when we have the necessary support from those we love.

Why is it then, that maintaining successful relationships seems to be the most challenging task? This book examines this question and provides a model for improving the relationships that are so vital to our success, health, and happiness.

Although I speak to thousands of people around the world annually, it took two years of concentrated effort to find 100 happy, satisfied couples—who had been together at least ten years—willing to take my anonymous online survey about their relationship.

It was interesting that many people thought their parents would qualify as a happy, satisfied couple, but when it came time to take the survey, the parents did not follow through.

There were times when one partner adamantly stated they had a happy and satisfied relationship but when I spoke to the other partner separately, he or she did not feel qualified to participate.

I did not give up my search for those happy, committed couples and eventually, with the help of many others, I achieved my goal of 100 couples taking my relationship survey. Do you want to know their secrets? That's what this book is about.

What I discovered from my search is that there are many people who are dissatisfied with their relationship. However they believe their mediocre relationship to be "normal" because all their friends are in similar relationships. I want to stress that just because a large number of people are not happy and satisfied in their relationships does not mean that you have to settle for mediocrity—that the relationship you have is as good as it gets.

I have reproduced the survey respondents took in Appendix Three and if you would like a copy of the advice respondents had for people about relationships, you will find this document free at www.InsideOutEmpowerment.com/HappyCouples/bonusgifts.html.

Admittedly, creating successful relationships with our significant others and parenting children are two of the most difficult jobs we will ever face; and yet we receive no formal training for either. The belief seems to be that people are born with the inherent ability to do these two things—yet, look around you. In the United States, the divorce rate is slightly over 50%! Only in baseball and basketball is a 50% average considered good.

Most couples get along when times are good. But when times are rough they fight with each other, ignore each other, or leave the relationship. Most people believe that seeking help with their relationship is an admission that they are flawed in some major way. They either view obtaining help as a defeat or they feel that their relationship is private and outside people shouldn't be brought into it, even to help. Still other people believe relationship counselors don't know any more than they do. After all, what's to know about keeping a relationship together?

The truth is that there is a whole lot to learn about having good relationships. Unfortunately, the only relationship training most of us ever receive is passive learning through the media or through modeling adults who live in our house when we are children. My models were my parents who received their informal training from my grandparents. My grandparents, in turn, learned all they knew from my great grandparents and so on back through the generations. This hardly qualifies as relationship training!

There is so much to learn about successful relationships that your parents never showed you. Please don't become one of the divorce statistics or perhaps worse, stay in a miserable relationship, honoring your marriage vows, while having regrets about your life.

On the surface, my parents appeared to have a very happy marriage. I learned from watching them that couples never argue, especially in front of the children. However my parents divorced right around their 25th wedding anniversary, contributing to that 50% divorce statistic cited earlier.

In some ways my training may have been worse than the training others received from parents who argued all the time. Disagreements are a natural by-product of relationships. It is impossible for two people to create a shared life without some of their ideals, values, opinions, or day-to-day activities conflicting with each other. The important question is how does the couple manage this conflict?

There are many considerations if you are part of a couple, regarding challenges and areas for growth and development in your relationship:

1. Do you know who you are as an individual? Does your partner?

2. Are you clear about the traits, qualities, and characteristics you are seeking in your ideal partner?

3. Are your life visions aligned?

4. Are your passions and purposes in harmony?

5. Do you share similar core values?

6. Are you able to smoothly cycle through the "Seasons of Love"?

7. Do you know how to find your ideal balance for interdependence within your relationship?

8. Do you know how to build each other up instead of tearing each other down?

9. Are you consumed by jealousy? Is your partner?

10. Is each of you satisfied with the amount, frequency, and variety of sex and romance in your relationship?

11. Are you engaging in effective communication? Or do you often have difficulty understanding each other?

12. Do you engage in proper problem identification?

13. Are you struggling to repair your relationship after an incident of infidelity?

14. Have you mastered the art of appreciating your differences?

15. Can you successfully manage conflict within your relationship by negotiating for a win/win/win outcome?

16. Do you know what it takes to maintain your relationship in good working order? Or do you only have the skills to acquire the relationship?

17. Do you know how to be true to yourself and your partner by blocking out negative, external influences?

18. Do you know how to survive the end of your relationship, whether it be through death, divorce, or a decision to separate?

These are some of the areas we will examine in detail in the upcoming chapters.

There is an expression that opposites attract. There may be some truth to this when considering the chemical interaction that occurs when two people meet and are attracted to one another. This chemical attraction doesn't care about values, personality characteristics, or hobbies. While chemical attraction plays a role in acquiring the relationship, compatibility—not chemistry—is a key for maintaining a successful, healthy relationship.

Another major consideration is how you relate to one another. Most of us were taught that if we use the Golden Rule everything will work out fine. The Golden Rule tells us to: *Do unto others as you would have them do unto you.* This sounds great and might actually be effective if the two individuals in an intimate relationship are an exact carbon copy of each other. How often do you think that happens? Never!

In relationships, people vary in multiple areas. What does respect look like? How do you apologize? What do you need when you are upset? What entices you to want to make love? What do you need when you are not feeling well?

You get the idea. There are so many areas where you and your partner may be different. The problem is that we continue to apply the Golden Rule, giving our partner what we would want in a similar situation, never realizing that what we are doing may be the exact opposite of what our partner wants and needs.

One of the main *Secrets of Happy Couples* is learning to apply the new and improved Platinum Rule®, a registered trademark of Dr. Tony Alessandra used with permission, which tells us to: *Do unto others as they would have you do unto them.* That's quite different from the Golden Rule. Can you see how its use would be far more effective in relationships than using the antiquated Golden Rule? In order to learn more about the Platinum Rule, please visit Dr. Alessandra's website at www. platinumrule.com.

Most people don't even realize that there are differences between them and their partner. People become so connected to their significant other that they often think they have the same minds; but this is not true. In order to engage the Platinum Rule, you must:

1. Recognize that there are differences between you and your partner.

2. Open up lovingly, without judgment, to explore what these differences are.

3. Determine if you have the inclination, patience, and resources to extend to your partner what he or she needs—instead of what you want to give in the situation.

4. Go ahead and actually engage in the behavior your partner would appreciate most.

Another area that often stops couples from working on their relationships is the faulty idea that it takes two. People believe they can't improve their relationship by themselves. This is simply not true. I do most of my relationship counseling with only one half of the couple!

Sound crazy? It's not if you subscribe to the tenants of InsideOut

Empowerment™. When I help people apply InsideOut Empowerment to their own lives, they learn two very important concepts:

1. The only person's behavior they can control is their own.

2. If they are unhappy, then they need to make some changes rather than sit around waiting for their partner to change.

When you practice InsideOut Empowerment, you don't give the power to anyone else to control your happiness, your moods, or your emotions. You know you are responsible for yourself and no one else.

What I often see with couples is that one person is unhappy with the relationship while his or her partner is fine with things. As a result, the unhappy partner postpones seeking help for the relationship, waiting for the other partner to recognize the need for outside intervention. People become filled with disappointment and frustration because their partner isn't the person they had hoped. They give away their personal power, waiting for their partner to change. In effect they are saying that they can't be happy in their relationship unless their partner does something different. This simply is not true.

If you are the one who is less than satisfied with the current state of your relationship, then do something! Take control of the one thing you can control, *you*—more specifically, your thoughts and your behaviors. Think or do something different that will bring you closer to the relationship you desire to create.

Your relationship is a system. Within a system, you can't change one part without it affecting all the other parts. If you make some changes, I guarantee your partner will change. It may or may not be in the direction you would like. However, you can increase the likelihood that you will get more of what you want by treating your partner the way you think he or she would most appreciate, thus increasing the odds your partner may improve the way he or she interacts with you. What have you got to lose?

You will learn to be the person you want to be—and to feel the emotions you want to feel—by changing how you think and what you do. The quote at the beginning of this chapter is representative of Inside-Out Empowerment. People and events will be what they are. There is very little you can do to impact other people's behavior and the uncontrollable events in your life. But there is *always* something you can do to better manage these circumstances.

The next two chapters are about the relationship cycle and learning how to negotiate each of its stages effectively. Sure you can do it through trial and error and maybe find your way, but the good news is that you don't have to anymore. You can benefit from what I've learned speaking to the experts and finding out their secrets.

Many success gurus say that if you want to be successful at something, you need to find someone who has already succeeded at what you are trying to do. That's what I've done. I've talked with 100 couples who have created the kind of relationship you have been searching for.

I recommend you read this entire book from start to finish. Think about all the ideas discussed and then choose one chapter, to start, that can really make a difference in your relationship. Make it something that you *know* you can do but will challenge you. Work on that area until you achieve a sense of accomplishment. Then go on to another chapter, repeating the same process, until you have created the relationship of your dreams.

Read on and then create your happy relationship. We're going to have some fun!

The Relationship Cycle:
The Alone Stage

Marriage asks more of its partners than does
any other relationship. At the same time,
it prepares its partners less for what could go wrong.

—Dr. William Glasser

Most books about relationships focus on either the Compatibility Stage—when you are deciding if you are compatible enough to make a commitment—or the Maintenance Stage—when you are attempting to figure out how to co-exist in a committed relationship over time.

Secrets of Happy Couples will focus on all four relationship stages:

1. The Alone Stage
2. The Getting Together Stage
3. The Compatibility Stage
4. The Maintenance Stage

It is my contention that a person's best chance for success in the Maintenance Stage comes with diligent care in the first three stages. While it may be possible to completely ignore the tasks of the first three stages and still achieve success in the Maintenance Stage, it is not likely.

The Relationship Cycle for Long-Term,
Committed Relationships

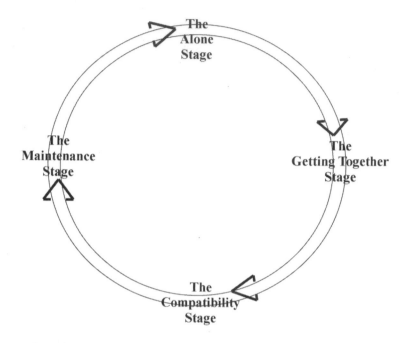

In this chapter we will focus on the first stage of the Relationship Cycle, the Alone Stage, since we cannot be happy in any relationship unless we are happy being alone. The chapters that follow will describe the other three stages and will bring them full circle. The reality is that all relationships end. Even if you are in a "happily ever after" relationship, the likely eventuality is that you will find yourself alone at some point. It is important to have the skills to cope with that eventuality.

Judith Sills, author of *How to Stop Looking for Someone Perfect and Find Someone to Love,* said, "The willingness to move to the next stage is the definition of timing."

Let's begin at the beginning.

Stage 1: The Alone Stage

Before entering a relationship, most people find themselves in the Alone Stage—the time period when they are between relationships. Although there are people who begin their next relationship prior to ending their current one and never experience the Alone Stage, it is less likely that they will experience happiness with their partner.

People predictably respond to the Alone Stage in one of three ways:

1. Some people look upon their time alone as a time to be depressed, angry, or lonely.

2. Others avoid being alone altogether by engaging in rebound and/or serial relationships.

3. And still others embrace their time alone as a time for reflection, contemplation, and self-growth.

Let's look at each of these responses separately.

Depression, Anger, and Loneliness: The people who respond with destructive emotions are fighting the situation that exists. Hale Dwoskin, in *The Sedona Method,* discusses that most human suffering is an inability to accept things as they are. There is no acceptance of the current state of aloneness. Many times people react this way because their previous relationship ended in a way they didn't want or expect. Their partner died, asked for a divorce, or made a decision to leave the relationship.

When people have been in a relationship with serious hopes for the future that did not work out because of death, divorce, or personal decision, the obvious response is to be sad, angry, or lonely. They had a vision of their future life with their partner and their hope was dashed. Many embark on this sad, angry, or lonely journey as their best attempt to continue the relationship. The person they wanted is no longer in their lives but they can relive the memories, thus maintaining some sense of the relationship in their current reality.

If they can't have the partners they want in their life, they can still think about them, wish for them, hope for their return, and mourn the loss of the life they planned together. While this is often a painful process, most people lack an alternative. This is the model they see in the media and in most of those around them: Boy dumps girl; girl is devastated. Girl cheats on boy; boy is crushed. Our culture does not provide healthy models of being in the Alone Stage. We have been conditioned to believe that a person is not complete without a corresponding "better half." This simply is not true.

Exercise: How to Turn "Lonely" into Simply "Being Alone"

Whenever you find yourself lonely and are feeling sorry for yourself, try any one or a combination of the following:

1. Use the time to take stock of all the things in your life for which you are grateful. You can always find many things to be thankful for, including having heat in your home, lungs that still breathe in and out, and food to eat. It is easy to forget these things while wallowing in self-pity.

2. Find someone in worse shape than you—you probably won't have to look very far—and then reach out to do something kind for that person.

3. Use the time to examine your own behavior to determine if you possibly have contributed to being alone and having no one in your life at this time. If the answer is yes, then make a plan to change some things in your life to make yourself more like a person others want to be with.

4. Reframe your alone time from "loneliness" to "my alone time" and do all those things you didn't do when you were in a relationship. Often, for the betterment of the relationship, you may forego certain things for the good of your partner or the relationship. Use this time as time to do those things that may not be conducive when involved with another person.

5. Create a social occasion for yourself. I remember once in college, I stayed on campus over the holidays to work. I was feeling sorry for myself, feeling separated from my family at that festive time. When I looked around, I found plenty of other people living on campus too. Since I thought they might be missing their families as well, I

planned a holiday party and invited people I noticed around. Most came. Nobody knew each other but a great time was had by all!

6. Engage in activities that are enjoyable for you. I like to take drives or get outside in nature to either walk or be still. Reading a book, a warm bubble bath, or journaling are also things that work for me. Try something you know works for you or experiment to find something new.

7. Reach out to people, far and near, whom you don't talk to often. Warm relationships with friends and family can help fill the void left by a significant other.

Remember, it's not being alone that's negative. It's the way you think about being alone that generates lonely, uncomfortable, and sad feelings. If you want to feel sad, angry, and lonely, go right ahead. There's nothing anyone can do to stop you. But if you'd rather feel better, or at least feel neutral, then do something different. Think of your alone time as a dormant time for rest, discovery, and rebirth.

Serial Relationships: Avoidance happens when you do anything and everything to not find yourself alone. People avoid being alone for a variety of reasons. Some people don't feel complete without a relationship in their life. Others do not like being without a sexual or an emotional partner to meet their needs. And still others head for a rebound relationship to attempt to manage their pain.

Neither of these approaches—engaging in serial relationships, or being depressed, angry, or lonely—is recommended for a healthy transition through the Alone Stage. Initially, grieving is an acceptable use of the Alone Stage but the key to a successful transition is what you do through your process and where you end up when you are through to the other side. With avoidance behavior, you may help yourself feel better temporarily but it may not be respectful of the person whom you are dating while you are rebounding. Also, you are not taking the time needed to examine your prior relationship so that you can take your learning into your next relationship.

People get into serial relationships because they don't take the time to learn the lessons from their previous relationships. The Law of Attraction is a simple law of quantum physics which demonstrates over and over again that we attract into our life that which we focus on. People who look at life and see positive, happy things will attract more positive energy into their life. When they look at life and see negative, unhappy things everywhere, then guess what? They are going to attract more ugliness into their life.

When they search for the relationship they want, they may focus on all the negative things in their past relationships. With such a focus, they will likely continue to attract more people with similar issues into their life. Taking the time to reflect when they are between relationships can help them avoid this pattern.

Embracing Time Alone as a Gift: What can you do with your time alone to turn it into a gift? First, remember you are perfect just the way you are. You are totally complete without a significant person to share your life. So often, in the Alone Stage, we focus on our lack, instead of our abundance. We look at the one thing we don't have, a romance, and waste the time we have been given feeling sorry for ourselves instead of using the gift of time for the betterment of mankind in our own unique way.

If you are interested in creating the relationship you deserve, then you must become the best person you can be. In my interview with author Arielle Ford, she said "When you're having a great life, that's when you find your soulmate." Each successive relationship you engage in provides you with lessons and information upon which to reflect. If you are attracting the "wrong" people into your life, then perhaps it is because you are not the person you need to be in order to create a relationship with the person of your dreams.

This also means that each "wrong" person you attract into your life is exactly the right person to teach you the lesson you need in order for you to move closer to meeting the person you truly want. This is why I never look back at any relationships I have had with regret. Maybe not in the moment, but over time I have come to understand that I learned valuable lessons in each of my past relationships which helped me become a better person.

Whenever you find yourself between relationships, it is not a time to longingly wish for the next partner to arrive. It is not the time to go out prowling for the next person to make you complete. The time between relationships is a very important healing time.

It's a time to learn to love yourself again, if you have forgotten. It is a time to take inventory. Make a list of all that you have to offer the world. What are your strengths? What are your interests? What are your talents and abilities? What do you love?

If you're having difficulty completing your list, ask someone you trust for help. An objective viewpoint can often point out positive attributes of which we are unaware.

And if, after taking this step, you are still unsure of your special talents and skills, then make a list of the person who you want to be. What would you like to be able to offer the world? Describe a person whom you admire and would strive to become. As long as there's breath in your body, it is never too late to learn to become the person that you truly want to be.

The Alone Stage is a time to look back on the past relationship to discover what that person was there to teach you about life, love, and yourself. It's a time of introspection to determine who you want to be in your next relationship. I'm not talking about playing roles; I am talking about a genuine transformation of yourself into the person who deserves the relationship you seek.

No one dreams their entire life about meeting a mediocre partner— someone who thinks of them *sometimes*, who loves them *a little* and takes care of *some* of their needs. No one desires to get involved in relationships with people who lie, cheat, and disrespect them. No one asks for verbal or physical abuse in a relationship. So how can we break the pattern of choosing the same type of person over and over again?

The key is to look at each relationship as the perfect relationship you needed at that point in time and then attempt to determine what made this person perfect for you during that period in your life. Once you figure this out, you will have learned a valuable lesson. If you take this lesson and use it in your life, then you will have one half of the equation.

The other half of the equation is about preparing yourself to be the kind of person who will attract the relationship of your dreams. If you are seeking a person to be loyal and to stand by you no matter what, then ask yourself the difficult question: *Do you possess these same traits and characteristics that you seek?* If there is something in your character that has caused you to be disloyal, then do some introspection to learn what you need to heal in order to become a loyal person who will attract a loyal partner.

Relationships act as a mirror, showing us the things about ourselves that we don't want to see. Welcoming the information and seeking to learn from it will move us closer in the direction of becoming who we want to be.

During this alone time it is advisable to create an inventory of the traits, qualities, and characteristics that you want in your "perfect mate" which you will fine tune in the Compatibility Stage.

Relationship expert, Dr. Karen Kan, has written an e-book entitled, *Creating Your Fairytale Love Life*, about using the Law of Attraction to attract the partner of your dreams into your life. You can find this book at http://lawofattractioninlove.com/products/ebook/.

Allow yourself alone time. Don't be in such a hurry to jump into the next relationship before processing the last one. Take time to analyze the lesson in your past relationship(s). Use your alone time to search introspectively to assess whether or not you are the person you need to be to allow the person you seek to come into your life. And finally, focus not on your lack of relationship, but rather on what you can do to help others during this time.

Used wisely, your alone time can truly make an incredible difference in the way you experience your next relationship. Don't short-change yourself. Maximize and leverage the time you have been given between relationships. It is truly a gift.

Rebecca

Rebecca is a 33 year-old woman who is between relationships. You will learn about her break up in the Compatibility Section of this chapter. For now I'd like you to hear about the lessons she has learned and continues to learn during her Alone Stage:

1. *I am enjoying singlehood and the freedom (time, space, and energy) it offers to explore my interests/hobbies, develop my career, make plans and create goals for my life, and strengthen my relationships with friends and family.*
2. *It's liberating to focus my energies on myself without the added pressures of a relationship and to self-care which can get neglected in couplehood.*
3. *I am not avoiding the grief and recognize the best way out is actually through. Being present and patient with the process...accepting that my emotions will ride like a roller coaster with ups and downs, sometimes in the same day.*
4. *I am looking at the relationship and subsequent breakup as lessons to be learned which will take me to the next great experience.*

Successful transition through the Alone Stage involves:

1. Resolution of the grief over your past relationship
2. Introspection into whatever role you may have played in the ending of the relationship
3. Taking stock of what you have to offer a relationship
4. Bringing into focus the qualities, traits, and characteristics of the relationship you desire to have
5. Becoming the authentic person you were intended to be so you can attract the relationship that you want into your life

Sometimes losing a relationship can be the best thing that can happen. If your partner chooses to go his or her separate way, then try to celebrate the fact that you discovered you were mismatched earlier as opposed to later. Know that you don't want to have your life tied to someone who is not happy and committed to you. Realize that no matter how much you love someone, it will never be enough to change a character flaw or make the person be the way you want him or her to be.

Understand that it's better to be alone than with the "wrong" person. This is the stage where you learn to be alright with being alone. Alone doesn't automatically equal lonely. You get to be introspective, correct some inconsistencies, and prepare for meeting the next teacher (your next relationship partner) in your life.

For more information on using the Law of Attraction to attract the partner of your dreams, please see Arielle Ford's book, *Soulmate Secrets*.

Chapter Two Summary

1. Relationships go through four stages: the Alone Stage, the Getting Together Stage, the Compatibility Stage, and the Maintenance Stage.

2. People respond to the Alone Stage in three ways: experiencing depression, anger, and loneliness; engaging in serial relationships; or embracing the time alone as a gift.

3. You can change being lonely into simply being alone.

4. The Alone Stage involves: resolving the grief from your past relationship; determining what role you may have played in the break up; taking stock of what you have to offer a relationship; bringing into focus the qualities, traits, and characteristics of the relationship you desire to have; and becoming the authentic person you were intended to be so you can attract the relationship you want into your life.

The Relationship Cycle
The Last Three Stages

*The most wonderful of all things in life, I believe, is the discovery
of another human being with whom one's relationship has a
glowing depth, beauty and joy as the years increase.*

—Sir Hugh Walpole

Stage 2: The Getting Together Stage

The second stage in the Relationship Cycle is the Getting Together stage:
how and where potential partners meet. People who don't like to drink
probably won't find their dream partner in a bar or club. People who aren't
very religious probably shouldn't look for their partner at the church.

When you are considering how to meet potential mates, think about
the person you want to date and ask yourself where he or she might
spend time. Someone recently asked me for a date in Blockbuster. Even
though I had to tell him that I am already in a wonderful relationship, it
made sense he would ask. He and I both love movies and he had seen me
in that store before. There was a common interest.

I always find it interesting to ask people who tell me they want to meet
their soulmate, what they are doing to find him or her. Often they tell
me they are doing nothing. And I really mean nothing: They go to work,
where they sit in a cubicle all day. Then they get in their cars and drive
directly home where they spend all their evenings alone. This isn't a great
plan for success, unless they plan to fall in love with the pizza delivery
guy or the checker at the grocery store.

Where to go? So what are some legitimate places to meet people? I was traveling one day and went to an Outback Steakhouse for dinner. I immediately phoned a single girlfriend to tell her I'd found where all the men are! There was table after table of men in large groups. From then on, we joked about finding men where you find good sirloin.

Many people are finding success with online dating, and I've even tried it myself. I believe this is a viable way to meet people, as the dating service will take care of matching you with others who theoretically are already compatible with you. I went through several lemons and some people I call friends before I found one person I dated for a short time. I caution people to take the time to get to know each other online prior to making plans to meet in person.

Exchange several emails and then begin a phone conversation before agreeing to meet. You can sift through several prospects in this way, avoid embarrassing situations, and possibly prevent some dangerous ones. Dating and relationship expert, Melody Glatz (SinglesDatingConvention. com), cautions that you haven't really "met" someone until you see them in person. An online relationship leaves out four of the five senses. The person could easily be claiming to be someone he or she isn't.

When you do decide to meet in person, always tell a friend your plans and have the friend call you midway through your date. Then phone your friend when you are on your way home. Glatz says:

> Use a safety call. A safety call is a way for you to check in with another person who knows where you are, whom you're with, and when you'll check back in. If you don't check in, or if you use a pre-arranged code phrase to indicate that you are in danger, your contact person calls for help.
>
> A good safety call is one in which your contact person has as much information as possible. Your contact should have the following information: your full name, your address, your phone number (home and cell), and details about your car (make, model, and license plate number), as well as your date's full name, home address (if you can get it), phone numbers, online ID, and any other information you have about him.

It's also very important to provide information about where you're meeting. Pre-arrange with your contact person when you'll call and check in. You definitely need to call them if there's a change in plans to another location. I like using text to check in. I send my first text when I arrive, another when I excuse myself to the ladies' room at some point in the date and then a text when I'm safely inside my home after the date.

Glatz says a better place to meet people with similar interests is at www.meetup.com. This is an international website designed to help people find others with similar interests. And it's free! You can find a group that meets around a variety of topics or activities, or start one of your own. This is a safer way to meet people because there is a group and the group is not designed to be a dating service. It simply provides people the opportunity to find others with similar interests.

If you are a single parent, you can often meet other single parents at your child's school activities. You will find other people interested in children and may be able to strike up conversations.

Should you go on blind dates? That is a personal decision. After my husband died, I had well-meaning friends who wanted to set me up with men I didn't know. I didn't want to rule anyone out but I also didn't like the pressure of a blind date. So, I would often ask if the potential date and I could be invited to a group event where we would get to meet each other to see if we were interested in dating.

If you are an avid reader, spend some time in book stores. If you are a computer wiz, spend time in cyber cafes. If you love to exercise, perhaps you'll meet your soulmate at the gym or the marathon you enter. I know a couple who met over a luggage carousel at the airport and have been happily married now for 27 years.

Many of my respondents indicated that they met the "right" person when they stopped being desperate to find someone to complete them. Usually it's when you stop looking that a potential suitor appears. Most people reported meeting their significant other through their regular daily activities or by introduction from a mutual friend.

I met the man I love, Marcus, through a mutual friend and it wasn't even a blind date! The three of us do similar work and our friend called together some workshop providers in an attempt to form a coalition of trainers in the Chicago area. The rest, as they say, is history. We've been together six years now and are very happy.

When you are emitting the right energy to attract the perfect person into your life, it will happen. However, why not help the Universe out a bit by making yourself available in places where you enjoy spending time? Even if you don't meet your soulmate, you may make some great friends along the way.

Successful transition through the Getting Together Stage involves:

1. Successful completion of the Alone Stage, moving beyond the desperation of *needing* to have someone in your life.

2. Making yourself open to meeting new people.

3. Finding someone with whom you'd like to explore a relationship.

Stage 3: The Compatibility Stage

Once you have successfully moved through the Getting Together Stage, you will enter the Compatibility Stage, where you determine whether or not you have enough in common to move toward commitment.

When you are seeking a life partner, you need to be clear about what it is you are looking for—what is important to you.

A few failed relationships in your past can help you narrow your focus, because they help you understand what you don't want from a partner. Then you can turn the "don't wants" into qualities and characteristics that you do want.

My 26 year-old son is currently yearning for a significant relationship but he keeps attracting women with low self-esteem and many insecurities. When I asked him what he was looking for, the only qualities he was concerned with were physical: body size, shape, and attractiveness. He really hadn't considered the other attributes that attracted him. Consequently, he has been attracting many beautiful, young women into his life, but no one has had the staying power because he is not clear about what he wants.

I suggested he make a list of all the qualities he wants in a woman, put it out to the Universe, and then trust that the Universe will deliver the right person at precisely the right time. Ms. Ford says both people in the relationship should make their "Soulmate List" separately and then they can compare them.

It is far more likely that you will attract the person you want when you become crystal clear about exactly what you are seeking. My list included having someone to love me for who I am, not in spite of who I am. I wanted a partner with loyalty, integrity, honesty, good looks, intelligence, a sense of humor, romance, and availability (not involved with someone else). I wanted a man who was strong but gentle, decisive but sensitive, and confident without being conceited. I wanted someone with whom I shared common interests and who didn't feel the need to control me or compete with me. Guess what? After I was clear about the qualities I was looking for and had done the work to have those qualities myself, I met Marcus.

Be flexible with your list but do not be willing to compromise so much that you don't even recognize the qualities you are seeking anymore. Divide your list into the following categories:
- qualities and characteristics you can't live without (deal breakers)
- qualities that are important to you
- the things that would be nice to have.

Achieve clarity of purpose.
Next, you need to take the time to explore what your partner wants in a relationship. This step is about asking the questions, listening for the answers, and watching for the demonstration of those answers.

Learning if your potential mate will match what you are looking for in a relationship should be motivation enough to ask the questions that need to be asked. Unfortunately fear can get in the way.

If you are desperate to have a relationship, then you may avoid the difficult subjects that could be deal breakers since the relationship feels so good initially. This is a common error in the Compatibility Stage. If you want to stop wasting time with incompatible people, then you need to ask the questions. Let's say you are opposed to having children but you are afraid to tell your date because you don't want the relationship to end. This is unfair to you both. You both have a right to what you want. When you want seriously different things, you are not right for a committed relationship. One or both of you will end up miserable.

It's possible that you may agree to continue spending time together while each of you is looking for the "right" person. I did this once and it was painful. I was involved with a younger man who had never been married. He really wanted to get married and have children. He knew I already had children and he wasn't interested in step-parenting. He wanted his own biological family. We weren't compatible for the long haul. However we enjoyed each other's company immensely and decided to continue to date each other while looking for Mr./Ms. Right. He found his first, which is what hurt me. I had to say goodbye but it was for the best. Now we both have what we want. He is married with two beautiful sons and I am with Marcus, who has already had his family and doesn't want more children.

While there is no magic amount of time to spend in the Compatibility Stage, remember that everyone looks good in the beginning. People in early relationship stages generally put their best foot forward, trying to make a good impression. They will often acquiesce quicker than when they are in an older relationship. Sometimes they even misrepresent who they really are.

Time is not the answer but what you do with that time is important. Watch your partner for signs of who they really are. Most people show us who they are but we refuse to believe them.

Sometimes your desire to make this person fit your list takes precedence over seeing who he or she really is. Occasionally people will show glimpses of what we want to see so we hang onto the hope that these glimpses are the true person's character underneath what he or she shows on a regular basis.

One thing I know for sure, marrying or committing to someone will not change him or her. Whatever traits you see now, will most likely be there later and possibly will even be magnified. What if he or she never changes? Will you still want to spend the rest of your life with this person? These are questions worth asking yourself.

The other extreme can also be true. You may have a partner who fits 95% of your list but your fear of settling for less than 100% can keep you from committing to that person. Generally, in human nature and in relationships, "perfect" doesn't exist. You can come close and learn to accept the rest. Sometimes people stay in the Alone Stage for a long time, because they are looking for perfection.

I interviewed author Judith Sills about what people need to do in the Alone Stage. She says the most important thing a person needs to do during the Alone Stage is to remain open to people and the possibilities of new relationships. Too often people in the Alone Stage are looking for that ever-illusive "perfect" partner. Perfection does not exist. In fact, many of the couples who agreed to take my survey initially responded with, "Well, things aren't perfect." Only when I assured them perfection in a relationship was not what I was seeking did they agree to complete the survey. They enthusiastically say they are happy and satisfied in their relationship but know that it is not "perfect."

Rebecca

When Rebecca was 31 years-old, she found herself in a two-year relationship that wasn't very compatible. She describes her live-in boyfriend at the time as a workaholic, which left her feeling lonely. He was frequently anxious about his work and emotionally unavailable. She stayed with him another year until she finally realized that John was not going to change. Once she realized that, her expectations of John and their relationship became more realistic. But she also grieved the loss of the dream of what could have been. She got all caught up in the glimpse of the man John allowed her to see and ignored who he showed himself to be on a daily basis.

Rebecca finally decided she would be better off alone than in a relationship with a guy who was all wrong for her. She is now back in the Alone Stage and is working on the following lessons:

1. Becoming conscious of what she really wants and not just how "shiny" a man can be.
2. Choosing someone not because of lust or convenience but because of his character and making character a priority.
3. Taking the time necessary to really know her next partner before making a long-term commitment.
4. No longer taking break ups personally. It's not that she needed to be "more" but rather that her partner was not able to give her what she needed.

Rebecca is committed to doing this work and will not settle for anything or anyone less than what she needs. She is doing the work of the Alone Stage.

Being flexible is critical but sometimes you can be as flexible as possible and still come to realize that this person is not a person with whom you want to commit.

Some people come into our lives for a reason, some for a season, and some for a lifetime. Trying to force a "seasonal" person to be a "lifetime" person is a mistake that many people make. This will never work.

Each person who crosses our path in an intimate way is someone from whom we have a lesson to learn. Value the lesson and when the time is right, allow that person to exit your life.

Attempting to hold on to someone who is incompatible with us in the important areas will result in suffering and heartache. Remember that an ending is always a beginning. You simply have to reframe your relationship. When a relationship ends, don't try to place blame. Understand that it has run its course. You have been shown important lessons and now this person must leave your life to allow for the next phase to begin. Embrace it. Learn from it.

Successful transition through the Compatibility Stage involves:
1. Knowing what you want in a relationship.
2. Taking the time to really understand what your potential partner wants from a relationship.

3. Staying firm and not settling for less on the important qualities, while remaining flexible on the qualities that are negotiable.
4. Distinguishing between when to commit and when to let go, and taking the appropriate action.

Stage 4: The Maintenance Stage

The stage not too many couples discuss is the last one, the Maintenance Stage. The Getting Together and the Compatibility Stages are relatively easy. That's where many people stop. They figure they've "won" the prize and now they can relax and coast. Wrong!

The Maintenance Stage is actually the most important of the four relationship stages: what you do to keep the relationship fresh, exciting, and loving. In my interview with Ms. Ford, she mentioned how important it is to keep discovering each other.

Relationships don't just run on autopilot.
• How do you hold your partner's attention?
• How do you continue to make your partner know he or she is special?
• How do you navigate the inevitable stormy seas that occur in committed relationships?

I learned from my survey respondents that one of the most important ingredients of a successful relationship is having a higher power, which could be considered God, the Universe, your Higher Self or your committed relationship. When individuals in a relationship focus selfishly on their own needs or masochistically prioritize their partner's needs, the relationship is not successful. Of the successful couples I spoke to, 34% mentioned having a higher power or prioritizing the needs of their relationship over their own individual needs. This point will be further discussed in chapter 15.

Another key to the Maintenance Stage is practicing the Platinum Rule, which was discussed in chapter 1. In relationships, people are taught to use the Golden Rule which states, "Do unto others as you would have them do unto you." The problem with this approach is that often males and females want very different things from their partner.

The Platinum Rule tells us, "Do unto others as they would have you do unto them."

When you stop providing your partner with the things you would want in a similar situation and instead focus on whatever your partner wants, you make great progress in the relationship department. Recognize that you and your partner want and need different things from your relationship. You may want love and affection, while your partner wants a hot meal at the end of the day. You may need reassurance when upset while your partner may need alone time.

Whatever the case, the application of the Platinum Rule involves taking the time to learn what your partner wants and then giving it to him or her. So often people maintain their relationship on autopilot by giving their partner what they themselves want from the relationship. This can work if you happen to want exactly the same things but more commonly it will fail, because the Golden Rule doesn't work in relationships.

The Maintenance Stage also involves open, honest, and respectful communication. Unfortunately fear usually gets in the way of such communication. You may fear the loss of the relationship or the consequences of telling the truth. First you need to get the fear under control by really examining it. Is what you fear really likely to happen? If it does happen, will you survive it? Are you willing to risk this relationship with dishonesty?

Once you have your fear under control, then you can communicate openly and honestly, allowing your partner into the inner recesses of your heart and mind. You free your mind, open your heart, and transform your life. True trust is about knowing that you are with someone who can see you with all your flaws and insecurities, and still love you.

In every communication, you must maintain respect for each other by following the Rules of Engagement you agreed to follow when experiencing difficult times, communication challenges, and differences. This will be explained further in the chapter on Effective Communication.

Successful implementation of the Maintenance Stage involves:

1. Making your relationship and/or your higher power a priority.
2. Learning what your partner needs to feel loved and providing it.
3. Communicating openly, honestly, and respectfully with your partner while minimizing or eliminating your fear.

Both the Compatibility Stage and the Maintenance Stage will be further discussed in subsequent chapters.

Chapter Three Summary

1. Relationships go through four stages: the Alone Stage, the Getting Together Stage, the Compatibility Stage, and the Maintenance Stage. The Alone Stage was discussed in chapter 2.

2. The Getting Together Stage involves: becoming open to meeting new people; moving beyond the desperation of *needing* to have someone in your life; and finding someone with whom you'd like to explore a relationship.

3. The Compatibility Stage involves: knowing what you want in a relationship; taking the time to really get to know what your potential partner wants from a relationship; staying firm and not settling for less on the important things; remaining flexible on the things that are negotiable; and distinguishing between when to commit and when to let go.

4. The Maintenance Stage involves: making your relationship or your higher power a priority; learning what your partner needs to feel loved and providing it; communicating openly, honestly, and respectfully with your partner while minimizing or eliminating your fear.

Developing Healthy Relationship Habits
What's Really Important

Beginning today, treat everyone you meet
as if they were going to be dead by midnight.
Extend to them all the care, kindness and understanding
you can muster, and do so with no thought of any reward.
Your life will never be the same again.

—Og Mandino

The habits we develop while interacting with each other are among the biggest challenges to maintaining healthy relationships. People generally learn how to relate to others from their family of origin and later from their peers and teachers at school. For centuries, parents, teachers, and other well-meaning adults have been doing their best to externally control the behavior of children. The relationship habits listed below have generally been considered acceptable and even necessary behaviors, when disciplining children. And they can render immediate, short-term results. Unfortunately, children learn and carry these Destructive Relationship Habits with them into their adult relationships.

In significant-other relationships, most people use some version of external control—one person attempting to get another person to do something he or she doesn't want to do. Naturally, there will be times when you want your partner to do something he or she doesn't want to do and vice versa. You may even try to get each other to do things neither of you want to do. And sometimes you will even try to force yourself to do something you don't want to do, simply to please your partner. The first scenarios are versions of external control; the last example is just a bad idea. For the most part they all result in misery for you and your partner.

The use of external control doesn't happen overnight. It is usually an insidious process, beginning without conscious awareness. People simply fall into a pattern of behavior that feels familiar to them. Human beings have been trying to control each other since the beginning of time.

Most people look outside of themselves as the cause of their unhappiness or frustration. After all, wouldn't life be practically perfect if the significant people in our lives would simply do things the way we want them to, or do what we think is best for them? Wrong! This is the kind of thinking that perpetuates the misery!

Most of the time people think they are unhappy because the important people in their lives are not cooperating with them. Can't you relate to that? Have you ever had children make decisions that put them in serious danger? Have you ever had a significant other make employment or financial decisions with which you were not in agreement? Did one of your parents ever say something critical to you that rocked your confidence? Ever had a supervisor who micromanaged your work and never gave credit for your good work performance? I think you get the idea. Any one, or combination, of these things can be a source of unhappiness for us. I'm sure you can add several others to the list.

Whenever we are in situations such as these, it sure *feels* as if our life would be so much better, happier, and more fulfilling if other people would just cooperate and be the way we want them to be. This may, in fact, be true. However the behaviors we typically engage in to move others in our desired direction are exactly the behaviors that damage, and ultimately destroy, our relationships.

I'm talking about the Destructive Relationship Habits: complaining, blaming, criticizing, nagging, threatening, and punishing. If we are particularly savvy, we can add to the list rewarding to control, otherwise known as bribing.

The pattern is perpetuated because sometimes it works. We can, in fact, get another person to do what we want through external means. When a person's pain exceeds their fear of change, they will change. It is possible to create enough pain for your loved one that he or she will do what you want. However you lose something very valuable in the process. You weaken the strength of the foundation of your relationship.

Use these Destructive Relationship Habits enough and they become ingrained. Our brain forms neural pathways that act like a default program on a computer. Whenever we aren't paying conscious attention, we subconsciously slip into the default mode of controlling others.

In order to have healthy relationships, we must become conscious and create positive relationship habits, while reducing or eliminating our use of destructive ones.

Destructive Relationship Habits

These relationship habits have been used since the beginning of time because at some point, somewhere, people decided that they had not only the right, but also the responsibility, to make others do what they wanted them to do.

One person in the relationship is not happy with something his or her partner is doing. This unhappy person then decides to engage in one of the Destructive Relationship Habits to "persuade" the other person to do what he or she wants them to do.

Martha and William

William had been experiencing some health problems and his physician had suggested he stop consuming alcohol. Martha was at the appointment when the doctor made this recommendation, which William is choosing to ignore. Naturally, Martha is disappointed by his behavior because she loves him and wants him to live as long as he can in good health. Every time William fixes himself a drink or orders one when they are out, Martha gets a dour look on her face, folds her arms across her body, or begins to slam things around. She thinks she is doing well by not criticizing him verbally. However her body language is still speaking volumes and what it is communicating is destructive to their relationship.

If these relationship habits are so destructive, why do people use them? The reality is they can work! Sometimes we can make situations so painful for our partner that he or she will cave under the pressure and do whatever we are demanding. This provides what behaviorists call intermittent reinforcement. Their research shows intermittent reinforcement to be the most effective motivator of behavior. What does this mean? When we try to modify a particular behavior and it is only effective some of the time, then we will use that behavior frequently, whether it gets results or not. However we will stop using a behavior that gets us what we want every time, the first time it doesn't work. This makes Destructive Habits an attractive choice.

What is the problem with Destructive Relationship Habits? Well, by definition they are destructive to our relationships. Even though we may get what we want in the moment, using a Destructive Relationship Habit will chip away at the foundation of our relationship. Is that what we truly want for the long haul? Yes, we can sometimes get compliance through the use of destructive relationship behaviors, but they will always weaken our relationship, creating either an overt or covert resistance to us and our requests. Is sometimes getting what we want in the moment worth the damage to our important, significant relationship? Probably not.

Perhaps you have never used any of the Destructive Relationship Habits. If so, pat yourself on the back because you belong to an elite club, perhaps a club of one. At different points in my life, I have used every one of these and occasionally still do so despite my efforts to stop. Let's take a look at these Destructive Habits that others have used with us. You may even notice one or two you've employed on occasion.

Dr. William Glasser and his wife Carleen Glasser, in their book titled *Getting Together and Staying Together*, talk about seven Destructive Relationship Habits. They are:

1. Complaining
2. Criticizing
3. Blaming
4. Nagging
5. Threatening
6. Punishing
7. Bribing or rewarding to control

Do you recognize any favorites of yours?

I like to add *guilting* to the list. This seems to be a favorite behavior of many mothers. I know, because I am one. You can recognize this pattern in martyr-type behavior, such as saying things like, "After all I've done for you, and you can't do this one little thing for me?" I've actually heard some mothers play the "childbirth card." You know the one. It sounds like this: "I was in labor with you for 36 hours! All I'm asking for is this one thing and you won't do it?" Guilting is actually a subtle, and sometimes not so subtle, variation on punishing.

Naturally, there are more Destructive Habits than the seven listed above—eight if you include guilting. However, if you begin by focusing on reducing just these seven or eight behaviors, then you will likely see a great improvement in the condition of your relationship.

Complaining: People use complaining when they are dissatisfied with a situation. People complain, expecting the other person to change and get on board with their way of thinking. How do you feel when someone complains to you or about you? Complaining is not a behavior that generally makes the complainer more attractive. Most people avoid complainers at all costs. And if the person complaining happens to be complaining about you, then it's even worse. No one likes to have someone complaining about them. It makes a person feel small and not good enough.

Criticizing: Criticizing is another behavior that is destructive to relationships. When most people ask, "What about constructive criticism?"

I respond, "Has there ever been a time when you were criticized and felt constructive afterwards?" The answer is usually "no."

Constructive criticism is an oxymoron. However, if people don't have the information they need to determine what quality work is, then I would hope someone would give them that information. I wouldn't call this criticism; I'd call it simply providing information.

Providing information is neither positive nor negative. It's just information. The core of who we are is not under attack. If we want something from our partners we need to tell them so they have the information to make their decision about whether they will comply with our wishes.

However, criticizing our partners' perceived character flaw or behavior is not recommended as a way of improving our relationship.

Blaming: People tend to engage in blaming whenever they don't want to accept responsibility for their own unhappiness. When we blame someone for something, we are attempting to point a finger away from ourselves onto our partner. "This is all your fault!" Or "It's all your fault we can't _____." (Fill in the blank with whatever you want.)

The reality is that whatever happened, happened. Pointing a finger in any direction does not change that reality. Instead of attempting to assign blame, it is more useful to go into problem-solving mode. How can the situation be salvaged? Given where we are in the moment, what is the next step to take? If the situation cannot be salvaged, there are three options:

1. Continue to blame
2. Make a note that you won't put yourself in that situation again
3. Forgive the person

Which choice(s) would be best for your relationship?

Relationship experts Drs. Gay and Kathlyn Hendricks at the Hendricks Institute, say that many couples are "addicted to blame, either of themselves or others." They suggest asking the question, "How did I contribute to this situation?" which changes the mindset from blame to wonder. You are wondering about your contribution instead of blaming your partner.

Nagging: Nagging is another Destructive Relationship Habit. If you have ever been on the receiving end of nagging, I'm sure you know how annoying it can be. When you've asked your partner to do something three times, you can assume he or she has heard you. The only logical conclusion is that your partner is not going to do it or will get to it in his or her own time. Asking another time is not likely to speed the process. Not only will it not speed the process but you can bet it will encourage your partner to pull away from you, damaging your connection.

Threatening: People threaten when they are trying to control their partner. It's a heavy-handed tactic designed to intimidate their partner into compliance. It usually sounds like, "If you don't do _____, then I'm going to *(do something painful to you)*." Sometimes the threats are simply implied but used for coercion nonetheless.

Do you think threatening and intimidation is healthy for an adult, intimate relationship? How can threatening strengthen a significant relationship? It can't.

Punishing: When threats don't work some people resort to punishing. Of course there are people who start with punishing, believing a threat might be wasted energy. They may think their partner already knows the consequences so threatening is a waste of time. When their partner engages in a behavior they don't like, they may automatically dole out the punishment.

Men and women, at least in the United States, seem to punish slightly differently. Since these are stereotypes there will definitely be exceptions. However for the most part, a man withdraws attention, and stops listening to his partner. A woman, on the other hand, withdraws affection, usually sex, and/or any words of respect or appreciation. These punishments can be quite effective because people usually choose to withdraw the one thing their partner wants the most. The partner often cannot stand the pressure and will cave under these circumstances. But if you are the person initiating the punishment, do you think your partner will feel closer to you afterward? Do you feel good knowing your partner only did what you wanted after you inflicted punishment? Is this the relationship you really want to have?

Bribing: Bribing, or rewarding to control, does not mean the same thing as negotiating. Negotiation in a relationship is very healthy and necessary to the long-term success of the relationship. Negotiation involves two willing participants, each interested in helping the other person get what he or she needs, while at the same time meeting his or her own needs. We will discuss negotiating under the Healthy Relationship Habits section.

Bribing simply means that I am going to dangle a carrot of what I think you want in front of you to get you to do the thing I know you don't want to do. Bribing creates resentment because it is experienced as a form of control and manipulation. No one enjoys manipulation, even if the reward is enjoyable. Albert Einstein said, "If people are good only because they fear punishment, and hope for reward, then we are a sorry lot indeed."

Tom and Julie
Being bribed can be demeaning. Tom and Julie's physical relationship had deteriorated to the point that they hadn't had any sexual activity in at least two years, despite being healthy and capable. Julie wanted her husband to put up a ceiling fan she had purchased for the living room. She told him she would be willing to have sex with him if he would put up the fan. After two years of no sex, Tom naturally wanted to create some intimacy so he installed the fan. However, when we were discussing the issue later, he finally told his wife how demeaning that was for him. Yes he wanted sex, but he didn't want it used as a bribe in their relationship. He resented her controlling him through sex, or any other means.

No one likes to be controlled no matter how subtly or skillfully the controlling is administered. External control is one thing human beings are almost guaranteed to rebel against. It's simple physics as exemplified in Sir Isaac Newton's Third Law of Motion: For every action there is an equal and opposite reaction.

Whenever people engage in a Destructive Relationship Habit, they are setting themselves up for similar treatment. Pushing someone creates the condition where that person has to push back. It isn't always directly confrontational, in your face. Sometimes it comes in the form of passive-aggressive behavior. But there is a push back or resistance created, nonetheless.

Wayne and Allison

An example of passive-aggressive behavior occurs in this story. Allison wanted Wayne to go to her company picnic with her. Wayne did not want to go to the party because he is not comfortable around Allison's co-workers. He is a mechanic and she is an upper executive in a computer programming division. His preference was to stay home to work on his car. However Allison didn't want to go to the party alone. Due to the long hours they both work, they do not get much quality time together.

Allison used some Destructive Habits and guilted Wayne into going to the party with her. Once they got there, Wayne hardly spoke to anyone. He was sulking the entire afternoon. Allison didn't have a good time because she couldn't relax worrying about Wayne. He made sure he acted in a way such that she wouldn't ask him to go with her to another company function again.

There are alternatives to using these Destructive Relationship Habits. There are ways to simultaneously honor yourself and your partner. The first step is to recognize when you are using Destructive Habits. Simply ask yourself if you are trying to get your partner to do something he or she doesn't want to do. Usually you will be able to recognize your use of Destructive Relationship Habits long before you feel equipped to do anything about changing them. This is natural. Of course, the best case scenario is that from this moment forward, you will never use another Destructive Relationship Habit, and will substitute a Healthy Habit instead.

If you aren't able to miraculously stop your use of Destructive Relationship Habits on demand, don't despair. Recognizing their use is the first step—bringing it into your conscious awareness. Once you are aware, then you can decide what you are going to do. Once again we can look to Albert Einstein and his definition of insanity: "Doing the same thing over and over again and expecting different results." In order to affect positive change in your relationship, you must try something different.

The Research

Since I have been teaching the principles of Dr. William Glasser's Choice Theory® for over 20 years, I was expecting my research to show that happy, satisfied couples have reduced the use of Destructive Relationship Habits and routinely employ the use of Healthy Relationship Habits instead. I wasn't disappointed.

I asked all couples to list the ingredients of their successful relationship —the things they consciously do to nurture their relationship. The top twenty items they listed included all seven of Dr. Glasser's Healthy Habits. Here's what made the top twenty. The Healthy Habits are highlighted in bold print:

1. Communication
2. **Respect**
3. **Trust/**Honesty
4. Time together/Quality time/Companionship
5. **Support/Encouragement**
6. Humor/Laughter
7. Prioritizing the relationship or one's partner over self
8. Commitment/Loyalty
9. **Listening**
10. Great sex
11. Common interests
12. **Accepting**
13. Shared spirituality
14. Similar beliefs and values

15. Time apart/Freedom to be one's own person/Individuality
16. Friendship
17. **Negotiation/**Give & Take
18. Having fun together
19. Physical touch/Affection
20. Understanding/Compassion/Empathy

To see the complete list of the Characteristics and Behaviors of Happy Couples, check out Appendix Four.

The Healthy Relationship Habits

Whenever you bring habitual behavior into your conscious awareness, you increase your options. Without conscious awareness, you are destined to continue the behavior which is motivated subconsciously. How can you stop what you aren't even aware of?

Now that you are paying attention you have more options:

• You can choose to continue using the Destructive Relationship Habits

• You can opt to say nothing

• You can engage one of Dr. Glasser's Healthy Relationship Habits.

In their book, *Eight Lessons for a Happier Marriage*, the Glassers write about the Healthy Relationship Habits of:

1. Listening
2. Supporting
3. Encouraging
4. Trusting
5. Respecting
6. Accepting
7. Negotiating differences

These are not as simple as they sound. Let's look at each one individually.

Listening: Listening is listed first because it may be the easiest place to start when trying to stop using Destructive Habits. You may already think you listen and perhaps you do. However the level of listening I am speaking of relates not just to hearing your partner, but truly trying to understand where he or she is coming from.

You are listening for understanding. You want to know how your partner sees things. You may not agree with his or her perception but you want to try to understand where your partner is coming from, as best you are able.

For such understanding, you must suspend your judgment about what your partner is saying. Approach the situation from a position of curiosity rather than judgment. Thirty-one percent of survey respondents said listening is an important part of their relationship.

Supporting: Supporting simply refers to standing by your partner, lending your support whenever needed.

Dennis and Rhonda

Dennis and Rhonda had vastly different vocational interests—he was a mechanic and she was a web designer. Dennis prioritized providing for his family. In the winter he heated his home with a wood stove, for which he chopped and stacked the wood himself.

Rhonda was very creative and was proud of the websites she designed for a wide variety of businesses. She would often call Dennis to the computer to see what she had done and he would respond with a very disinterested, "That's nice, dear." He, in turn, would call her to their basement to see the great woodpile he had stacked, and she would be annoyed to have to go downstairs to look at a bunch of wood. Neither was supporting the other.

It's easy to be supportive when your partner is doing what you want. It's more challenging to be supportive when doing so may create difficulty for you. This is either a time for negotiating (discussed below) or supporting your partner and then determining what you need to do to also get your needs met.

When you are supportive you recognize your partner's accomplishments and support him or her when things are challenging. Thirty-nine percent of survey respondents listed support and the next habit of encouragement as central to their relationships.

Encouraging: I have been asked, "What is the difference between encouraging and nagging?" Well, there's actually a big difference. When you encourage people, you are encouraging them to do something they already want to do. When you nag them, you are encouraging them to do what *you* want them to do. Big difference!

Encouraging is for times when your partner needs a cheerleader. He or she is considering something that could potentially bring great joy but might just need a little encouragement to carry it through.

In order for you to be a helpful encourager, you need to control your own fear about whether things will work out. You may worry if your partner does a particular thing, that it will somehow take him or her further away from you or endanger your happiness in some way. While this is possible, when you can be the encourager it is more likely that your partner will move closer to you.

Sometimes your fear of losing your partner is something that keeps you from using Healthy Relationship Habits. This fear comes from a place of illusion. Your partner is never yours to own. Yes, in marriage you make promises. You want to believe those promises will last a lifetime. But the reality is that people are free to come and go in our lives. The tighter you try to hold onto someone, the greater the likelihood that he or she will leave.

Even if you are successful in getting the person to stay, do you really want a relationship based on guilt and obligation? Sometimes the Healthy Habits seem counterintuitive because we have been raised to believe in external control. But know that every time you use Destructive Habits, you are weakening the strength of your relationship.

Trusting: Of the happy couples surveyed, 49% said that trust was crucial to the success of their relationship. Many of us come into relationships with baggage from previous ones, possibly making it difficult for us to choose to trust. Many say trust is earned. However I believe that if you have made a decision to be in a relationship, then you must also make the decision to trust, until you receive information to the contrary. Trust is a true gift in a relationship.

If you've exercised poor judgment in the past, instead of using that as an excuse not to trust, begin to think of it as a situation that helped you develop more discriminating instincts. When you learn to trust yourself first, it becomes easier to trust others.

If your partner betrays your trust, then put your trust in your higher power. Know that you will survive and actually be stronger for the experience. You have learned a vital piece of information.

After the betrayal you will have decisions to make about your relationship. Not all relationships end when trust has been breeched. Some couples can overcome dishonesty and even infidelity, by finding their way back to trusting each other again. In fact, of the couples taking my survey, 13% indicated that one or both had had an affair. Their relationship survived and even became stronger as a result. These will be decisions you will need to make if and when your trust is violated. But don't let someone else's lack of integrity define you. Your partner is only human and will make mistakes. Infidelity may be one of them. Don't let that mistake make you feel that you are somehow "less than"—as if you're not good enough or are a fool for trusting. Trusting your partner is the way to a healthy, satisfying relationship.

Respecting: Respect is a very interesting concept. In a relationship, you should never do anything that demeans or reduces your partner's self-esteem. This is typically caused by the Destructive Habits of criticizing, blaming and complaining, which should be avoided at all costs. However there is more to respecting than avoiding these Destructive Habits. Many will tell you that if you follow the Golden Rule, then respect will be the byproduct; but I disagree. The Golden Rule says, "Do unto others as you would have them do unto you." This implies that respect looks the same for all people and this is not the case.

Let's take, for example, a simple yet common difference between men and women. Typically, when a woman is upset about something, she needs to vent, often talking about her issue over and over again. She is not necessarily looking for a solution, but simply needs to process the issues out loud. If her partner knows how to respect her, he will let her vent as long as it takes while listening for understanding.

On the other hand when a man is upset about something, he usually needs to retreat somewhere within himself to figure things out. Since talking helps the woman feel better, she will frequently nag her partner to tell her what is bothering him. In order to truly respect her man, she needs to give him the space he needs, and trust that he will come back when he is ready.

In the area of respect, I once again recommend following the Platinum Rule: "Do unto others as they would have you do unto them." This will require more "listening for understanding" to realize what respect means to the other person. Fifty percent of respondents listed respect as an important part of their relationship, second only to effective communication.

Accepting: Acceptance is one of the more challenging habits. I always say you have at least three options in a dissatisfying relationship: You can change it; accept it; or leave it. When you are attempting to change it, there are usually two ways to do it. Most of the time, you try to change your relationship by getting the other person to change so you can be happier. This is when you will likely engage in the Destructive Relationship Habits.

A more productive way to improve your relationship is to change yourself, which happens when you implement the Healthy Relationship Habits. If your attempts to change have been unsuccessful and you don't want to leave the relationship, then accepting is what is left available to you.

Accepting means that you accept traits, characteristics, and behaviors in another without resentment. Holding onto your resentment is simply another way to try to change the person. Acceptance sounds like this: "I am choosing to stay in relationship with you because that is what I want. I recognize that you are not perfect, just as I am not, but the positive greatly outweighs the negative. I know this is simply a part of you and I accept you fully and love you exactly as you are." Getting to this place with a loved one is truly a beautiful thing. Of the happy couples taking my survey, 29% mentioned complete acceptance of their partner as a critical aspect of their relationship.

Negotiating Differences: It is unrealistic to think you can be in relationship with anyone and not encounter differences. Using the Healthy Habits does not mean you need to be your partner's doormat, constantly giving up what you want in favor of what he or she wants. No, being in a committed, healthy relationship means you both figure out win/win/win solutions for the two of you to get what you need—where you win, your partner wins, and your relationship wins because it is strengthened by going through the process.

To determine a win/win/win solution you take turns sharing with your partner what it is that you want. You both listen for understanding. You talk about placing the good of the relationship above either of your individual needs. And then you figure out a way you can both get what you need in the process.

The key to negotiating differences is that there is no coercion for any specific behavior change from either partner. The negotiation is a freely given gift to the relationship. You both must be willing to place your own individual needs on the back burner, while negotiating what is best for your relationship. Twenty-one percent of respondents to the survey listed negotiation as an important behavior in their relationship.

Where to Go from Here

This chapter has been geared toward the relationship with your significant other. However the principles discussed are universal principles. They can be used in any relationship. You can implement the Healthy

Relationship Habits with your children, your parents, your in-laws, your siblings, your co-workers, your supervisor, strangers, yourself—basically anyone in your life with whom you'd like to get along better.

I have one word of caution. If you commit to using the Healthy Relationship Habits and want your partner to do so too, you must guard against the natural inclination to say, "I'm doing this and I think you should too." The reason to use Healthy Relationship Habits needs to be because it will be great for your relationship regardless of what your partner does. This is not a situation where you should say, "I'll do it if you do." Make your changes from a pure place and your partner won't be able to help but be affected.

However, depending on how long your relationship has been less than supportive, it may take longer for your partner to notice your efforts. Don't despair. Keep doing what you know to be right for your relationship. Things will improve. You can't help but feel more loving toward a person who is intentionally trying to love better.

Take the first step. Start using the Healthy Habits and you might be amazed at what happens. If you would like a free list of The Destructive and Healthy Relationship Habits to post in your home, go to www. InsideOutEmpowerment.com/HappyCouples/bonusgifts.html.

Chapter Four Summary

1. People have been using Destructive Relationship Habits since the beginning of time.

2. You can get short-term immediate results with these Destructive Habits.

3. Destructive Habits can be quite subtle and even non-verbal.

4. Destructive Habits become habitual with use. Destructive Habits chip away at the foundation of our important relationships, gradually destroying them.

5. The Destructive Habits are: complaining, criticizing, blaming, nagging, threatening, punishing, and bribing.

6. People do not like to be controlled and they will actively or passively resist.

7. The happy couples surveyed agree that the use of the Healthy Relationship Habits help to make their relationships stronger.

8. The Healthy Relationship Habits are: listening, supporting, encouraging, trusting, respecting, accepting, and negotiating differences.

9. Choose the Healthy Relationship Habits because it is the right choice for your relationship, not because you are trying to get your partner to use them too.

What Do You Need?

Know Thyself and Thy Partner

Understanding human needs
is half the job of meeting them.

—Adlai Stevenson Jr.

What do you argue about? What are your disagreements? The small resentments? What do you have to give up to get along?

Do you argue over money? Are you fighting over sex? Do you disagree about the fun activities in your life? Do you have different ideas about how much time you should spend together and apart? Do you squabble over extended family and friends? Is one of you daring and reckless, while the other wants to play it safe? Does one or both of you need to be right all the time? Does one of you want to always be in control? Couples may have conflict in many areas.

Do you know that there is a simple explanation for the conflict and a corresponding solution? When looking for a life partner, it is a good idea to take a close look at your Need Strength Profile, based on the work of Dr. Glasser and his theory of human behavior called, Choice Theory. I have been a student of Dr. Glasser's for over 20 years and have found these concepts central to a couple's relationship and ability to get along with each other.

This chapter discusses the five basic human needs of Choice Theory:
1. Love and Belonging
2. Survival, Safety, and Security
3. Power
4. Freedom
5. Fun

We all have them; Dr. Glasser theorizes that they are genetically programmed at birth. However, each individual experiences these needs to varying degrees. Let's examine these five basic needs.

Love and Belonging

Love and belonging determines how much connection you require with others and how important it is for you to feel that you "belong." This encompasses your need for intimacy, romance, sex, time with friends, your connections with family, the drive you have to belong to different groups, how much you want to be liked, and how much you want to minimize conflict. This need will help you determine as a couple how much time you spend together and how much time you need apart.

People with a high need for love and belonging in a relationship want to have a lot of quality time with their partner. They generally like to be physically close and enjoy a high degree of intimacy. People high in love and belonging may have many friends or a few very close friends, but they enjoy relationships with others. They are most comfortable with people they know.

People who have a low need for love and belonging do not require this type of closeness or time with others. They generally like to spend more time alone and have difficulty understanding the point of increased intimacy.

Generally speaking, relationships work best when partners have similar love and belonging needs. When there is an imbalance in this area, one partner is asking for more quality time, while the other is seeking space.

Survival

The need for survival is mostly physiological, involving such things as food, air, shelter, exercise, good health, and reproductive sex (for survival of the species). However it also encompasses the need to feel safe and secure, which is more psychological than physiological.

People with a high need for survival are quite uncomfortable with change. They like to be prepared for any eventuality. They don't typically buy on credit but pay cash for purchases, and like to save. They are not risk takers. When diagnosed with a terminal illness, they will do everything within their power to prolong their lives. When the new millennium came and people were concerned that the world was going to end, those with a high survival need were totally prepared. They had the generator, canned food, bottled water, and money, probably in the form of silver and gold coins. People with a high need for survival will do whatever is necessary to protect themselves and their own.

On the other hand, people with a low need for survival generally live in the moment, can accommodate change quite well, are not concerned with debt, are more of a spender than a saver, and like to take risks.

An imbalance in the need for survival, where one partner has a low need while the other partner has a high need, can strain the relationship. One appears to be fearless, while the other may be afraid of even minor change. One is spending while the other is in agony over the degree of debt accumulated. While one is preparing for every eventuality, the other is seeking spontaneity in the relationship. Areas of potential conflict around this need involve the ability to adapt to change, spending and saving money, preparing for safety, risk-taking, and spontaneity.

Power

Power can be a difficult need to understand because it generally has a negative connotation associated with it. When people hear "power," they often think of one person exerting power over another. While this is one way to meet one's power need, there are two other ways which are more responsible, palatable, and socially accepted.

There are three ways to meet one's need for power: power *over* others, power *with* others, and power *within* oneself.

Power Over Others: When people have a high need for power, they are born driven to get this need met. They don't know how to get it met; they just know that they must find and maintain power. If you observe small children at play, you will often see the tendency to power *over* others. When two year-olds are playing together and one wants the toy the other is playing with, he or she will generally take it. If the first child won't give up the toy, then the perpetrator may hit, kick, bite, or in some way hurt the child in his or her best attempt to get the toy.

When I say it was the child's "best attempt" to get the toy, I don't mean that there wasn't another way. Rather, I am saying the child hadn't experienced another more effective way. Children who never learn another way to get their power needs met grow to be the bullies on the playground and/or the bosses who take credit for others' work. These people get their power need met regardless of, and sometimes because of, the effect it has on other people. They will continue throughout life to "power *over*" others in order to meet their power need.

Power *over* others is not a responsible way to meet one's power need because it interferes with the other person getting his or her needs met. There are plenty of people who use power *over* others but this is generally not the best way to achieve harmony in personal relationships.

Hopefully life teaches children the other two ways to seek power, so that they can get their power need met without interfering with others meeting theirs.

Power With Others: People who meet their power need by "powering *with*" others are able to work cohesively with a group of people to advance toward a common goal or objective. Many winning sports teams, as well as effective work teams and even fully functioning families, display this "power *with*" concept. Power *with* others can be a very satisfying way of meeting one's power need; however it requires the cooperation of others to be successful.

Power Within: Power *within* oneself is generally seen as a need for competence, having an impact, and recognition—things people are good at, proud of, or have accomplished in their lives. Those with a high power need who meet it through "power *within*" like to always do their best. They may seem to be perfectionistic but producing their best is very need-satisfying for them.

The need for power has a big influence in interpersonal relationships. It plays a part in workaholism, perfectionistic tendencies, and low tolerance for imperfection in others. People with a high need for power are frequently seen as "control freaks."

When people have a high need for power, they like to be right; they want to be competent and recognized; they are ambitious and seek success in their ventures. Being respected is important to them. When people have a low need for power, they do not need recognition being generally content to work behind the scenes without any glory or accolades.

Having both partners with high power needs can be challenging to a relationship. One person trying to power *over* the other person causes problems in relationships. Each wants to make the decisions and have the last word. Both want to be right.

On the other hand, if both partners have a low need for power, then power will most likely not be a factor in their relationship, except to the extent that they may have difficulty getting things accomplished.

Relationships work best when both partners have a moderate need for power or one partner has a higher need for power and the other person a relatively lower need for power. This latter combination can be a recipe for a healthy relationship as long as the person with the high need does not become abusive toward or take advantage of the partner with the lower need. But even in this best case scenario, different strengths in the power need can be problematic if a couple is attempting to reach a common goal and the one with the high power need is very goal-oriented while the other partner appears more lax in that area. This scenario also has the potential of creating a type of hero worship.

Power *within* can also be problematic in relationships when both partners have a moderate need for power or the person with a high power need, who meets it through power *within,* expects the same behavior from his or her partner, and does not understand their differences.

Two people with a high power need can make their relationship work if they find a project upon which to collaborate but clearly delineate the areas of control for each person. Another way their relationship can work is if they satisfy their power need solely through work and check it at the door when they come home. This would be an example of making a seemingly incompatible situation work.

Freedom

Freedom involves the ability to do things one's own way; breaking rules, particularly the ones that don't make sense; a need for time away from others; and the ability to do what one wants when one wants without restriction.

People with a high need for freedom are independent and need to do things their own way. They have difficulty asking for help. High freedom-need people generally do not like rules—particularly ones that don't make sense. They also value their time alone. They like to do what they want, when they want.

There is usually an inverse relationship between the love and belonging need and the freedom need. People with a high need for love and belonging, typically have a lower need for freedom, and vice versa. Of course there are always exceptions.

People with a high need for freedom are free spirits. They are often highly creative. They do as they please. They are sometimes viewed as selfish because they generally move through life as they want, without regard to others' feelings.

People with a lower need for freedom easily accept being told what to do, welcome rules, and do not have a great need to be independent.

It can be challenging for a relationship when one partner has a high need for love and belonging while his or her partner has a high need for freedom. With this combination, one partner wants closeness and time together, while the other partner craves space and time apart. It's easy to see how this could produce some conflict in the relationship.

If both partners have a high need for freedom, the relationship can work. Both partners will generally do their own thing, without any negative repercussions for the relationship. And when they come together, things are good.

When both partners have a moderate need for freedom, they will have a mixture of activities together and apart. As long as there are not certain activities for which one partner wants companionship while the other tries to avoid that activity, this will be a healthy combination. Finally, when both partners have a low need for freedom, they are quite compatible in this area and probably enjoy a lot of quality relationship time together.

Fun

Fun seems pretty straightforward but there are some subtleties that one must understand.

There are basically three kinds of fun. There is the loud, energetic kind of fun that people might get from joking, physical activity, and parties. There is the quiet, relaxing kind of fun that might be enjoyed by fishing, lying in a hammock on a warm summer's day, or reading for pleasure. Then there is learning as fun.

Dr. Glasser says fun is the genetic reward for useful learning. When people engage in something they want to learn that has immediate, useful applicability to their own lives, it is fun. For me, the best example is when I learned how to downhill ski and made it the first time down the slope without falling and getting snow down my jacket, up my pant legs, and various other places! It is the sheer joy of learning and mastering something that interests you.

Therefore, people with a high need for fun may look like one of these three types: a joker, someone who is always laughing; a person who likes to engage in lots of quiet leisure activity; or a person who doesn't seem on the outside to be having a lot of fun but is studying and learning a great deal. People with a low fun need do not appear to need a lot of time engaging in any of these activities.

For the success of the relationship, it is best when the strength of your fun need is similar. If one person seeks fun excessively, while the other person has a relatively low need for fun, then the first person thinks the other is boring, while the other is wondering if his or her partner is ever serious about anything.

If two people have a low need for fun then they will be compatible in this area. Similarly if they both have a moderate or high need for fun, they will be compatible along this line.

In addition to the strength of their fun need, it is helpful if partners enjoy some of the same types of fun. Everyone has various ways of meeting their fun needs; it is these differences that can drastically affect the couple's satisfaction in their relationship. If one partner is always seeking the loud, energetic kind of fun, while the other is looking for the quiet, relaxing kind of fun, then it may be difficult to find activities they can enjoy together.

Therefore it isn't always about need strengths. Sometimes the incompatibility comes from the various methods, behaviors, and experiences people choose to meet their individual needs.

Consequently, it is important for couples to find ways to meet their fun need together. This doesn't mean that they must enjoy exactly the same things for the same reasons. I know couples who have found creative ways to have fun together. Greg likes to go fishing. His wife doesn't fish but she enjoys going in the boat with him and reading a book. There is another couple I know, where the wife likes to photograph the outdoors and the husband enjoys hiking. The important thing is for couples to find ways of having fun together and develop common interests.

A final note: there is an interesting interaction between the five needs, too many interactions to enumerate here. I'll just give one example. If you are in a relationship where both of you have a high freedom need, then you may never have conflict around the fun need. Because of your high need for freedom, you give each other a lot of space and often engage in your fun activities alone or with others. When this happens, you are each free to engage in whatever fun activities you choose without being concerned about whether or not your partner wants to do them too.

There is so much to learn about improving the significant relationships in your lives! Need strength compatibility provides one more piece to the puzzle.

Need Compatibility Quiz

Answer each question with the first thought that comes to mind. Ask your partner to do the same. Add up the total points for each section and record your totals below in the spaces provided at the end of the quiz.

Survival

I am extremely conservative.
Less True— 1 2 3 4 5 *—More True*

I save rather than spend.
Less True— 1 2 3 4 5 *—More True*

I take very few risks.
Less True— 1 2 3 4 5 *—More True*

I have a strong distrust of new things, ideas, and people.
Less True— 1 2 3 4 5 *—More True*

I exercise daily and eat well for good health.
Less True— 1 2 3 4 5 *—More True*

I really hate change of any sort.
Less True— 1 2 3 4 5 *—More True*

Love & Belonging

I greatly enjoy time spent with other people.
Less True— 1 2 3 4 5 *—More True*

I am a member of many different groups.
Less True— 1 2 3 4 5 —*More True*

I really hate conflict.
Less True— 1 2 3 4 5 —*More True*

Relationships are very important to me.
Less True— 1 2 3 4 5 —*More True*

I am only comfortable around people whom I know.
Less True— 1 2 3 4 5 —*More True*

I love romance and loving sex.
Less True— 1 2 3 4 5 —*More True*

Power

I have a lot of skills and abilities.
Less True— 1 2 3 4 5 —*More True*

I always seek to do my best in everything.
Less True— 1 2 3 4 5 —*More True*

Leaving a legacy is very important to me.
Less True— 1 2 3 4 5 —*More True*

I need to be right most of the time.
Less True— 1 2 3 4 5 —*More True*

I like being recognized for my accomplishments.
Less True— 1 2 3 4 5 —*More True*

I must always have respect from those around me.
Less True— 1 2 3 4 5 —*More True*

Freedom

I am extremely creative.
Less True— 1 2 3 4 5 —*More True*

I feel very frustrated when I believe I don't have any choices.
Less True— 1 2 3 4 5 —*More True*

I always question the rules.
Less True— 1 2 3 4 5 —*More True*

I really hate being told what to do.
Less True— 1 2 3 4 5 —*More True*

I enjoy a lot of time to myself.
Less True— 1 2 3 4 5 —*More True*

I must do things my own way.
Less True— 1 2 3 4 5 —*More True*

Fun

Learning something new is always enjoyable.
Less True— 1 2 3 4 5 —*More True*

I laugh oftcn.
Less True— 1 2 3 4 5 —*More True*

There are many hobbies that I enjoy.
Less True— 1 2 3 4 5 —*More True*

Even when things are supposed to be serious, I find myself making fun.
Less True— 1 2 3 4 5 —*More True*

I can turn drudgery into fun.
Less True— 1 2 3 4 5 —*More True*

Making others laugh is my mission in life.
Less True— 1 2 3 4 5 —*More True*

Partner A record numbers from above here:

Survival	Love & Belonging	Power	Freedom	Fun
_____	_____	_____	_____	_____

Partner B record numbers from above here:

Survival	Love & Belonging	Power	Freedom	Fun
_____	_____	_____	_____	_____

In summary, for the compatibility of relationships, it is best when you and your partner share similar need strengths for love & belonging, survival, freedom, and fun. It also works well when you have a dissimilar need strength for power, particularly if the way you meet that need is by powering over others, including your partner.

After you and your partner have assessed where each of you are in terms of these needs, share your scores with your partner. Be open to listening if your partner has a different interpretation and see if what he or she says makes sense to you. If you see validity in the input, then adjust your score accordingly.

If this discussion has gone well so far, then you may begin to analyze with each other where there may be some problem areas in your relationship. This chapter is just designed to get you looking at yourselves and how each of your need strengths is currently affecting the relationship.

In accordance with what you learned in this chapter, congratulate yourself on the areas in which you are compatible. When you discover areas of possible incompatibility, begin a discussion about whether or not you have conflict in that area. If you don't, it is likely you have found successful ways to manage the difference. If you do, then you can discuss ideas for managing these differences in a healthy way that strengthens your relationship.

Chapter Five Summary

1. Everyone is born with the five basic needs of Love & Belonging, Survival, Power, Freedom, and Fun.

2. Each of us has some needs that we experience more strongly than others, creating a unique "Needs Strength Profile."

3. Knowing which needs are high for you and which needs are high for your partner are two pieces of the puzzle for a quality relationship.

4. Understanding where need-strength incompatibility may cause conflicts in your relationship—and knowing what to do about it—will help you strengthen your relationship.

What Do You Want?
Asking the Tough Questions

Lust is when you love what you see.
Love is when you lust for what's inside.

—Renee Conkle

When you are in the Getting Together Stage, you might have the tendency to just sit back and enjoy the journey without actively seeking to discover if this person you are spending time with is truly compatible with you. There is nothing wrong with this approach if all you are interested in is dating.

If, however, you are interested in moving your relationship forward toward a deeper commitment, then you need to leave the Getting Together Stage and move into the Compatibility Stage, where you do the exploration necessary to determine if you possibly have what it takes to stay together for the long haul.

When two people first explore a relationship with each other, they must consider several things. Unfortunately, most couples get caught up in the chemistry of the relationship and don't attend to the foundation upon which they are standing to determine if it is strong enough to support them as a couple. That foundation is built upon vision, mission, and values.

We discussed what you need in the last chapter. Now it's time to examine what you want and then explore whether your partner wants the same things. There will be things you want that have nothing to do with your partner. There will be things you want that would be nice if your partner wanted too. And finally, there will be things you want that are essential to the happiness of your relationship with your life partner.

It is important to examine these essential things to determine relatively quickly whether or not your partner shares similar vision, mission, and values.

When you determine incompatibility early in your relationship, you can let go of that partner and move forward toward the person you really want. Settling for the person in front of you simply because you've already invested time in the relationship is no guarantee of lasting happiness. In fact, it often guarantees the opposite.

This is the time when you have to get clear about what you really want, communicate these desires to your partner, and determine if your partner is on the same page with you—or at least in the same book!

When people are in the Compatibility Stage, they may talk about how many children they'd like to have but rarely do they discuss their beliefs about discipline or how they might approach challenging situations with their children.

People seem to have the mindset that they do not want to "rock the boat" in the early stages of their relationship by bringing up topics about which they may disagree. The goal seems to be to "hook" the other person—to gain that commitment—with the thought of confronting the difficult situations as they arise, when perhaps the risk of losing the relationship is diminished.

Given the over 50% divorce rate in the United States, it seems only too obvious that simply making a commitment is not enough to keep a relationship intact. Even those couples that stay together may do so simply because of the commitment or because of the children or because of the expense of getting divorced. Do you want to end up in a relationship where your partner is only with you out of guilt, finances, or obligation?

One way to increase the odds that you will have a solid relationship is to check its foundation prior to making your commitment. While there are no guarantees, assessing and discussing your vision, mission, and values will help determine if you can potentially be happy for a lifetime with your partner.

What the Research Shows

In my research, I asked happy couples how happy they were in the following areas with their partners: financial, relational, mental/intellectual, physical, and spiritual. The results were interesting. There were often one or two areas where these satisfied and happy couples were not satisfied and happy. However, the areas where they weren't happy with their mate were either areas that weren't important to them or they were areas where they had other ways to get that need met.

Fifteen percent of the couples taking my survey thought that having common goals was important to their relationship success. Forty-seven percent said spending quality time together was important; 29% reported having common interests was critical; and 23% said sharing similar beliefs and values contributed to their relationship success. These areas represent the relationship's vision, mission and values.

Vision

Not everyone has a vision for their life but many people do. A personal vision is where you want to be at some point in the future. The more specific you can be about that vision, the more likely you will realize it.

When two people come together to create a shared life, it is most helpful if their visions can blend. Imagine a couple where one partner's vision involves living in a cabin in the mountains of Montana while the other partner envisions a large home in Charleston, SC. Or a couple where one person is very interested in the accumulation of wealth and living a fast-paced social life while the other wants to live simply and privately. These are relationships destined for unhappiness. Without discussing visions, unhappiness is a strong possibility.

Similarly, if you have no vision, you may find yourself lead into a life you don't want, thus creating unhappiness for yourself.

Take time to figure out what you want for yourself and your family. Get as clear about your desires as you possibly can, knowing they will be shaped and molded by your experiences.

A vision is just that, a vision. Visions can change. You aren't locked and committed to a vision you created in your 20s. However it is helpful to spend the time clarifying what you want and then learning if your potential life partner has a vision that will blend with yours.

Mission

People who are unclear about their mission in life generally do not succeed. Discover your mission so that you will have greater success. Your mission is the same as your purpose. Your purpose is what you were put on this Earth to do. Every person was placed on this Earth for a reason. There are no spare parts. Each person has something unique and valuable to contribute to the world, thus making the world a better place.

Some people are aware of their purpose early on. I knew in fifth grade that I wanted to be a counselor. I was, in essence, the counselor for all my friends in fifth grade. People came to me for advice. I had great listening skills and was highly empathic from a very young age. I recognized my gifts and embarked on a path to share these gifts with the world.

Others go to their grave not knowing their mission. They may never have asked the question, "What is my mission or purpose here?" They may buy into a paradigm about work that has nothing to do with enjoyment. Some people do what their families or communities expect them to do, never listening to their inner voice urging them toward their mission. Still others allow fear and doubt to take them off the path of living their purpose.

Living your purpose is actually the topic of another book. However as it relates to couples, knowing your mission and communicating that to a potential life partner can help you determine your compatibility.

I know a couple where the husband is a doctor and the wife is a nurse.

They have mission—compatibility in that they are both in the field of health care and believe in the western medical model of healing. With this simple connection they have much in common.

Imagine another couple where one partner is the owner of toxic landfills while the other is an environmental activist whose mission is to clean up toxic waste. Or imagine a couple where one is a vegan, aspiring to prevent the slaughter of animals for human consumption, while the other raises beef cattle for high-end steak houses. Can you imagine the dinner conversations these couples will have? They will either sound like WWIII or there will be complete silence. Once the anger is spent, there is nothing left to say. Pretty soon these "partners" will simply stop talking to each other.

Knowing your mission and the mission of your partner will help you determine whether or not you will be compatible.

Values

What is important to you? Make sure you let your potential partner know. This is not a time for guessing games or assumptions. If something is important to you, please have the discussion.

When working with clients, relationship experts Beth Banning and Neill Gibson stress the importance of people distinguishing between their core values and the strategies they employ to experience these values. By using tools such as their Values Exercise (available free from www. FocusedAttention.com/resources), they encourage people to develop what they call their Values Intelligence™.

Values Intelligence is your ability to easily determine the underlying values that generate your personal preferences and motivate the actions you take in the different situations in your life. But more importantly, it is your ability to consciously choose the actions you take to ensure that they are in harmony with your core values.

One way you can practice this ability is to consider each of the following situations and pick the one you most strongly identify with. Then use the Values Exercise to identify the underlying values that generate your preference for whichever strategies you might choose.

What if you believe in saving for a rainy day and your partner believes that money is meant to be spent? What if you like to show love by giving lots of gifts and your partner perceives this as bribing? What if you believe in non-physical discipline of children and your partner believes that the only way to discipline children is through their behinds? What if you are highly social and love spending time with people and your partner is a bit of a recluse?

One key thing to remember is that while core values—such as harmony, honesty, fun, loyalty, etc.—are never in conflict, the set of values that seem most important to one person in a specific situation may be very different than those that seem most important to someone else in that same situation.

Without recognizing the underlying values that motivate each person's preferences in a given situation, the situations listed above have the potential to create conflict in a long-term committed relationship. The time to discover these latent conflicts is now, not after the commitment.

Donna and Darren

Donna and Darren encountered a serious conflict in the way their values were expressed after being married over ten years. They were raising two boys, and while they didn't always agree on issues related to the children, they believed that they shared similar value systems. Some of their values included honesty, hard work, family, and commitment. They had been having some difficulty with their older son telling lies and were working with him to correct that behavior.

One Halloween, Donna took her boys to a neighbor's house trick-or-treating. The neighbor asked them if they had seen her cat. Donna's oldest boy made a very audible sound of "uh-oh." When the neighbor asked what he knew, the youngest boy hit his brother and the boy replied, "Nothing."

Once they had left the home, Donna asked what was going on. Well, apparently, Donna's brother-in-law had shot the cat, mistaking it for a stray. This is apparently not uncommon in places where hunting is a sport. After the boy's uncle realized his error, he told the boys, "Don't you tell anyone"!

The next day, the neighbor cornered Donna's son as he was getting off the school bus. He confessed what his uncle had done and the neighbor became furious.

When Donna told Darren what had happened, he was angry. Donna couldn't understand his reaction. She was proud of their son for telling the truth because the value of honesty was very important to her in this situation. Darren was angry because the boy's actions had embarrassed the family; the value of loyalty was more important to him.

While both Donna and Darren valued honesty and family loyalty, it was important that they recognized which value they held in highest esteem in this unusual situation. There are probably many other values that played into this situation for both Donna and Darren. But without the ability to discover each other's values, and then to identify ways to move forward that respect all of them, it's likely that this situation will become an ongoing conflict.

Of course you won't be able to anticipate every possible conflict in the way your values may be expressed. However thinking about common challenge areas and identifying your underlying values in each of these areas can help prevent later problems from developing.

I really enjoyed James Arthur Ray's book, *Harmonic Wealth*. In it he divided life up into the five categories I mentioned: financial, relational, mental, physical and spiritual. It's important to get clear about what your values are in each of these areas and then discover your potential partner's values.

The following sections provide some guidance in these five areas. The lists below are not exhaustive, nor are they offered for you to grill your potential partner with every one of these questions. Determine the questions that are of importance to you. Use my questions or create your own. And then, without fear, begin a conversation with the intention to discover the core values each of you holds in these areas. Should you determine that the two of you are incompatible, wouldn't you rather know now, as opposed to later, after you have invested more time?

Financial: Money matters have been blamed for many divorces in this country. Do some preventive work by ensuring that you are on the same page with your partner in matters of finance.

Are you a spender or a saver? When you invest, do you prefer low, medium, or high risk investments? What is your position on credit cards and savings? Who do you think should manage household money? Do you want finances to be separate or together? Is it all right to not pay all your bills on time? Are you a proponent of allowances? How do you make decisions on big-ticket items? Is it important to be honest about your expenditures?

Where does work fit into your daily priorities? How many hours do you anticipate spending at work each week? What sacrifices are you prepared to make to advance in your career?

Do you want to own or rent your home? How important is it to own a new vehicle? How do you budget and what are the priorities? If one of you were granted a promotion in another geographic area, would the other move? How often do you want to go on vacation? Where do you want to go? How much money will you allocate? Do you prefer new things or finding ways of making due with what you have? Do you collect things? If so, what is the extent of your collection?

Relational: Relationships outside the couple unit can enhance or create stress for your relationship. It's worthwhile to discuss these ahead of time to determine where each of you stands on these important issues.

How do you get along with each other's extended family? What do you believe about caring for elderly parents? How involved do you want to be in your partner's life and activities? What are your thoughts on spending time with each other's family and/or friends? How much time do you think is reasonable for your partner to spend with friends without you? Do you always think you should be included when your partner spends time with friends? Do you enjoy time with each other's friends? When is it all right to prioritize relationships outside of your committed one? What are your thoughts about sharing your relationship problems with outside people? How do you and your partner feel about relationships with the opposite sex? How much personal space or alone time do you need when things are going well and when they aren't?

What are your beliefs about child rearing? Do you and/or your partner want to take time off when a child is born? Do you expect your partner to leave his or her job to provide child care and if so, for how long? What type of childcare arrangements do you foresee having? If something happened to both of you, who would you want to raise your children? How involved do you want to be in your children's life and activities? What values do you want to instill in your children? Is it important to present a united front to your children even if you disagree? If there are step-children, what will the parenting look like? What are the relationships with the exes?

How do you want to spend your free time while not at work? Where do fun activities fit into your priorities? What do you like to do for fun? How do you feel about company coming to your home? How much time do you think you should spend with each other? How much time can be spent apart? What does quality time look like for you and how important is it to your relationship? Are there things you really want your partner to do with you? Are there things your partner wants you to do with him or her? Do you enjoy these things? Are there things you definitely do not want to share with your partner? How does your partner feel about that?

What are your thoughts about pets? Will they live in the home or outside? Whose responsibility will they be? What takes precedence: family, work, or leisure? How do you each allocate your time in these areas? What are your standards for housekeeping? Are you generally a giver or receiver? How does this mesh with your partner's style?

Mental/Intellectual: If mental and intellectual pursuits are important to you and you want to share them with your partner, then you need to ask some of the questions below to determine your compatibility in this area.

What are your thoughts on self-development and education? Is it important to have intellectual discussions with your partner and if so, is he or she your intellectual equal? How much time, energy, and resources will you devote to mental pursuits in your relationship? Is it important to be of the same mind on certain issues? If so, which ones?

When is it OK to tell a lie? Do you consider deliberate omission a lie? Do you think you need to consult each other on every decision you make? If not, when is it OK to make an independent decision? When you are upset, do you like to talk about things or figure things out on your own? What type of communicator are you and does that mesh with your partner's style of communication?

Do you ever apologize and if you do, what would warrant it? When you are trying to figure out a problem, whose opinion do you seek first? Do you believe that having good manners is important? Is a sense of humor important to you and if so, what type of humor do you usually engage in?

Where do you stand politically? What is your position on diversity and equality? How do you balance work and fun? What do you think you have in common with each other? How green are you? Is it important that your partner is eco-savvy? Do you conserve electricity, water, fuel, etc? Do you recycle? Do you support local area businesses? How important are these values when raising children?

Physical: For some individuals, the physical component of a relationship is very important. If you are one of these people, you need to determine how important it is to have your partner value the physical aspects of your relationship too. If that is important to you, then these questions can help.

How important is health and physical activity? Do you prioritize health over other things? Does your partner? Do you exercise? If so, is it important for your partner to work out also? Do you want to do this together or is it all right to have separate routines? Are you into health food? Do you go to the doctor and for what? What is your stand on drugs, alcohol, and smoking? How much alcohol use represents problem drinking to you?

How important is physical appearance to you? Do you have issues with getting or looking old? How will you handle it in yourself and your partner? When is extra weight an issue and what do you do about it? How would you handle your partner gaining weight? What would your expectations be? Where do you stand on caring for a terminally ill family member? If you or your partner requires physical care, how would each of you handle it?

What are your sexual interests and fantasies? What are your feelings about public displays of affection? Do you think monogamy is critical to the health of your relationship? How often and in what variety do you want to engage in sexual activity?

Spiritual: Is religion or spirituality important to you? If so, is it important for your partner to share the same or similar beliefs/values? To what extent? What are your religious or spiritual practices? These are all questions you want answered before committing to a long-term relationship.

When is it appropriate to attend religious functions? What do you think about religion and the raising of your children? What happens if one of you outgrows the other spiritually? How much time, energy, and resources do you want to allocate to this area?

Overall Goals and Direction

Another critical piece to consider is whether or not you have similar ideas about your overall goals and direction in life.

Spiritual advisor and coach, Marcus Gentry, says the single, most important factor in a couple's relationship is not how they look *at* each other but rather to what degree they are standing together side by side looking in the same direction.

A less serious, but nonetheless important, consideration is vacation time. One couple I know, Laurie and Matt, have very different ideas about what to do with their one week vacation each year. She prefers the luxury and social opportunities of cruises or resort locations, while he prefers the quiet and solitude of a fishing cabin in the woods. They resolve this conflict by taking turns each year.

Vacations are not much of a problem since they only involve a few weeks a year. But what about couples who can't agree on where they want to live? I know a couple who lives in Chicago. Desiree works for an insurance company that offered her a big promotion but she will have to relocate to Texas. Her husband is proud that she got such a great offer but can't stand the thought of living in such a hot climate.

Another couple with whom I've worked had a disagreement involving family commitment. Mark was very ready to take a step in the commitment area by having a child with Theresa, but Theresa did not want to have a child until she and Mark got married. This resulted in a stalemate and their eventual breakup. It emphasizes another conflict in goals and direction.

Sometimes you find a partner who is very compatible with your need strengths and your values but has different ideas about how to meet goals.

I remember in my own marriage, both my husband and I were compatible in the area of family values. We both prioritized family and family issues very highly. However the prioritization looked quite different for each of us. For me it meant that when I was done with work, I would seek out the company of my husband and children—whether that was at home, on the baseball or soccer field, or at the wrestling gym. I simply wanted to be where my family was. My husband's idea of prioritizing family meant that I would go home after work and prepare a family meal that we could all enjoy together.

While you may be reading this scenario and agreeing with either my position or his, the point is that neither of us was wrong. We simply had different pictures of how to display our family values. This idea of right and wrong often gets in the way of couples resolving their challenges. Each person becomes convinced that his or her way is the right way and that the other is wrong. People in conflict often seek out people who share their view, thus solidifying the attitude that they are right. Once this attitude takes hold, it becomes increasingly difficult to find ways to negotiate and compromise.

You and your partner may completely agree on your values in terms of how much responsibility and how much freedom you will allow your children. But when it comes down to implementing these values, you may find, to your surprise, that you completely disagree about specific responsibilities and freedoms that you want to extend. You may be completely comfortable allowing complete freedom with driving privileges, while your partner is more comfortable with dating privileges. Again, it is important to remember that all disagreements about strategies are most easily resolved when you take the time to discover the values that are important to each of you that are not being honored by the conflicting strategies.

Often when you are becoming involved with another person intimately, you aren't talking about your combined goals and direction. If you do, you are either talking about what you want to accomplish in a year or in your lifetime. Somehow the in between part is lost.

I was recently speaking to a couple who happens to be very good at planning their goals and direction together.

Rick and Katie

Rick and Katie were telling me that they had recently purchased a house. They had moved out of northeast Philadelphia and bought a home in New Jersey. Rick proudly told me that they are on the five-year plan. In five years they plan to move into a new neighborhood so that their oldest son can attend a better school. Together they have decided what they want for their lives right now, in the long-term, and everywhere in between. They basically have five-year goals. They created this harmonious path and are walking it together.

If you are considering entering a committed relationship with someone, it will be very beneficial to complete the following exercise. It will help you discover if you are aligned for the long haul. If you are already in a committed relationship, then completing this exercise will help you determine if your paths are similar. If they are not, it is time to determine if you can negotiate certain things for the good of your relationship.

It is difficult for some to think far into the future. According to the experts at the University of Oxford, the molecules of the human body change every seven years. It is unlikely that what you think you'll want in 20 years will actually be what you want 20 years from now. The idea is to go through the exercise to see if there are any real deal breakers you can foresee in your future. Also, if you are not seeing your current love interest as part of your future planning, then that tells you something about your current relationship. Perhaps it isn't meant to go the distance.

Naturally, your plans can be adjusted. You are not rigidly committed to anything you write down. All plans are flexible and you have the right to change your mind. However, after making plans in conjunction with your partner, you owe it to him or her to communicate when your plans and/or commitment level have changed.

When creating this combined vision for the purposes of goal setting and attainment, I suggest that you begin at where you want to be toward the end of your life and work your way backwards. All the goal setting gurus I have studied recommend Stephen Covey's approach of "beginning with the end in mind" and then working backwards to more short-term goals. If you are conscious about where you want to end up, then you can more easily plan what has to happen between now and then to make these end goals a reality.

If you are completing this goal exercise simply to determine if you and your partner are in alignment, then it really doesn't matter where you begin. You can begin a year from now and then work your way forward.

Complete your forms individually, and then get together to compare what you have created. Completing the forms independently increases the likelihood that you will both express your dreams and desires from your hearts without outside influence. From that starting point, you can then negotiate where you want to go as a couple. Your love for your partner may cause you to alter your answers to be more in line with his or hers.

Goals Exercise

Take a sheet of paper and write down your goals in the following areas. Do one for one year, three years, five years, ten years, 20 years, 30 years and so on. Then compare these with your partner's goals. Look to chapter 15 for how to negotiate the differences.

_____ Years From Now in the Year 20____ :

Physical Goals:

_____

_____

Financial Goals:

_____

_____

Relationship Goals:

_____

_____

Mental/Intellectual Goals:

_____

_____

Spiritual Goals:

_____

_____

People will either grow together or apart in relationships. Change is the only constant. People are living longer. A life commitment made in a person's 20s can easily mean the next 60 or even 70 years! For your relationship to thrive, you must learn to renegotiate your relationship. Just because you've changed and your changes feel completely right for you, doesn't necessarily mean that they will be right for your partner.

For your relationship to survive, you need to accept your partner and his or her changes. If your partner can no longer satisfy certain things that he or she did in the past, then find someone or something else that can. This does not mean you need to end the relationship or have an affair. You may find a friend who can do the things your partner can't or doesn't want to. Find an outlet for those needs. Join a group. Make new friends. Read some books. Don't look to your partner to share your enthusiasm for that part of your life when he or she has changed goals or direction.

However, if your partner's changes are completely unacceptable to you, then you may decide to end your relationship. Do so without anger or resentment.

Chapter Six Summary

1. When in the Compatibility Stage, prior to making a commitment, it is important to discuss your vision of the future and your life purpose to determine whether or not you are aligned and compatible.

2. Check out each other's values in all areas that are important to both of you. Look specifically at the financial, relational, mental/intellectual, physical, and spiritual areas. Determine if you match.

3. Determine your overall goals for the next 20 or 30 years.

4. Assess in what direction you are looking and if you believe it is a shared direction.

5. Accept your partner's changes along the way unless they are changes you can no longer live with. Then make a decision about whether or not to continue the relationship.

Seasons of Love
Discovery, Support, Challenge, Renewal

Love is shiny when new, and bursting with color.
Strengthening with time, it grows and then one day
becomes even more beautiful than when it began.

—Flavia

Long-term committed relationships follow the pattern of the seasons and then the cycle begins again. The length of your relationship and the experiences you have shared determine how many seasons you have been through.

Discovery occurs during the spring. It is when couples are exploring each other, delighting in the discovery of new things. Summer is associated with support and autumn with challenge. Winter is a time for regrouping and renewal. This is a time when couples regroup from the challenges of autumn and find their balance again.

Dr. John Demartini, in *The Breakthrough Experience*, writes about love as being a combination of support and challenge. Without both, love is lopsided and flawed. Most couples I surveyed mentioned some combination of support and challenge in their relationships. Although support is associated with summer and challenge with autumn, these can occur during other seasons as well.

The Spring: Discovery

When a couple first gets together, it is springtime. They are discovering each other for the first time. Everything is new.

This season can be both awkward and exciting. You are getting to know a new person. When the discovery is fun and you appear to be compatible, it is very exciting. If you have many differences or conflicts early on, you may choose to end this relationship in the spring.

Most people in the spring of their relationship put their best foot forward. They are nice, kind, polite, attentive, and interested in the things the other person likes. They want this new person to like them.

The spring usually feels great and often leads into the summer.

The Summer: Support

During the summer season, couples are spending more and more time together. They enjoy each other and share many things. Their relationship is progressing and they are very supportive of each other. God help the person who speaks against their partner!

What does support look like? Support is being someone's best friend— seeing their faults and loving them anyway. Support is being positive about the things your lover wants to do, even if they don't include you. Support is listening to your lover's hopes and fears. Support is keeping your partner's secrets. Support is being your partner's coach and biggest cheerleader. Support is providing a place of refuge for your partner, a place where he or she can find peace.

So what if your loved one wants to do something and it affects you in a negative way? How do people stay supportive when their partner wants something that they don't want him or her to do? These are some real life examples.

Multiple Examples:

I remember being very impressed with my son's fiancée in the early part of their relationship. My son wanted to go out of town to visit his brother at college over the weekend. Now this wasn't any ordinary weekend—it was

Valentine's Day. And she gave him her blessing. She was only 16 at the time but I thought she was incredibly wise when it came to relationships.

A friend tells a story about wanting to go to his family reunion out of town. His family didn't have annual reunions so this one was quite special and he was really looking forward to it. However, his wife was not going to be able to accompany him on the trip. He still wanted to go but his wife asked him to stay home with her since she couldn't go. He reluctantly agreed to stay home and regrets it to this day. That was over 15 years ago! As an aside, he is no longer married to that person.

Another friend called me not too long ago to say her husband made a decision to go out of town with his father to do some work for 10 days. Guess when it happened to be? You guessed it—over Valentine's Day. The woman was unhappy about him going. It meant she would be alone for Valentine's Day. Her workload would be increased because now she would have to care for their daughter alone. However, she sent him away with her blessing.

Steve, a newlywed, recently returned from Iraq. When he learned that his unit was going to be deployed again, he decided to re-enlist. His wife, Christine, was not pleased about this decision. She was pregnant and knew he would most likely not be home for the birth of their first child. However, she also understood the value of support. She said, "This is what Steve loves. He could never be happy staying behind when people he cares about are going back to war." Though young, Christine understood the value of support.

When you truly love someone, you support his or her goals and direction even when what your partner wants conflicts with what you want. You certainly have the right to ask for what you want. But once the decision is made, you need to support it even if it isn't what you asked for.

Know that your significant other isn't doing what he or she is doing to intentionally hurt you. People generally do what they do because it meets their needs. Does that mean you aren't important? Absolutely not! It just means that your partner has needs that may have nothing to do with you.

If you truly believe your partner is deliberately trying to hurt or disrespect you, then why are you with this person in the first place? It may be time to make a change.

The happy, satisfied, committed couples who responded to my survey commented on the importance of having the unconditional support of their partner. They know they can do whatever they need to do and their partner will support them.

I am not talking about being someone's doormat. However when your significant other wants to do something and you stand in the way, do you think that strengthens or weakens your relationship? Do it often enough and you won't have a relationship. Or worse, your partner will become the person you want and lose him or herself in the process. After that kind of soulless transformation, you will likely lose interest in him or her.

Take responsibility for meeting your own needs. If your partner decides to do something when you were hoping for something else, determine what need would be met for you if your partner did what you want. Then create a plan for you to do something that will get that need met in a responsible way.

Love is the unconditional support of another. Unconditional support means that even if your loved does something that you don't like, you'll be supportive anyway. It really isn't about you.

I'm definitely not talking about letting your partner treat you badly. I am talking about supporting the person you love in the things that are important in his or her life.

If your partner's work is important, then appreciate the time and energy it takes to invest in it. If time alone is important, then allow the person the time he or she needs. Even if the person decides you are not "the one" for him or her, allow your partner to move on in his or her life without interference from you.

This is the definition of real support in a loving relationship: to be your partner's personal cheerleader and/or coach.

The Autumn: Challenge

The autumn season brings challenges to overcome. After the smooth sailing of the summer, autumn introduces new conditions into the relationship. Some possible relationship challenges include moving, the birth of a child, job or career changes, financial stressors, an affair, caring for elderly parents, children leaving home, or death.

Some relationships cannot survive these challenges and couples separate. Other couples stay together but separate emotionally. Successfully navigating the autumn season means you face the challenge together, get through it, and emerge stronger on the other side.

One area of challenge occurs throughout all the relationship seasons: the challenge of holding your partner accountable for being the best he can be, particularly in the areas in which he would like to be successful. Challenging your partner is always done in private and in a loving, supportive way. If you think your partner is wrong about something, ask him to explain his thoughts. Remember, you still may not see things in the same way based on your individual values, perceptions, and experiences. The goal is to seek to understand even if you disagree.

If there is something your partner wants to do but lacks the skill or confidence, be encouraging. Encourage your partner to be the best he can be, particularly in those areas in which your partner wants to excel. Do not encourage him to be a doctor so your standard of living can improve when your husband wants to be an auto mechanic. Don't encourage your wife to be a stay-at-home mother when what she wants is to continue her law career.

Two Couples

Malcolm and Kate are a happy, committed, interracial couple. He always wanted to expand his solo vocal career. Up until that point, he sang bass in several different groups but that did not showcase his vocal agility and talent. Kate bought him some musical equipment and encouraged him to form a band and create his own solo show. He is now a successful R&B solo performer.

Joel and Jennifer are a successful couple. Jennifer has struggled with her weight her entire adult life. Joel is very supportive of the person she is, never criticizing her body size. Whenever she decides she wants to join a gym or begin a new diet, Joel challenges her to maintain her program. If she is less than successful, he supports her unconditionally again. He has mastered the art of balancing support and challenge in his love relationship.

The Winter: Renewal

Winter is a time for renewal. After the challenge of the autumn season, it is time to regroup and restore your relationship's equilibrium. If you have successfully navigated the challenges of autumn, then you and your partner need a dormant period to reconnect and to assess how you are different—individually and as a couple.

Going through the challenge of autumn has its effects. You will likely be changed by the challenging experiences. Your relationship's equilibrium will be disturbed and you will need quiet time as a couple to determine the new parameters and balance of your relationship.

Some couples will get through autumn and find that they don't have any basis left for a relationship. They will reenter the Alone Stage. Other couples will come through the challenge of autumn and become stronger.

Once they reestablish the balance in their relationship, they will reenter the spring season of discovering who they are now, after going through their respective changes. It can be an exciting time again.

And the seasons repeat, over and over again, for as long as the couple remains in a long-term committed relationship.

When you consider the Seasons of Love, what season are you in and which mindset does it require: discovery, support, challenge, or renewal?

Chapter Seven Summary

1. Long-term committed relationships follow the pattern of the seasons and then the cycle begins again.

2. Spring is the season of discovery.

3. Summer is a season of support.

4. Autumn is a season of tests and challenges.

5. Winter is the season of renewal.

Becoming a Couple
Dependence, Independence, Interdependence

In the progress of personality, first comes a declaration of
independence, then a recognition of interdependence.

—Henry Van Dyke

An imbalance on the Dependence/Interdependence/Independence Continuum can create challenges in a relationship. As we explore this continuum, it will become clear that there is no ideal position to occupy. Rather, each couple must find their own unique position of equilibrium that works best for them.

The Dependence/Interdependence/Independence Continuum

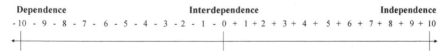

Dependence	Interdependence	Independence
-10 - 9 - 8 - 7 - 6 - 5 - 4 - 3 -2 - 1 - 0 + 1 + 2 + 3 + 4 + 5 + 6 + 7 + 8 + 9 + 10		

Dependence

Let's begin with dependence because that's where we begin in life. At birth, people are necessarily dependent upon their caregivers to provide all their needs. Without their caregivers babies and young children would die.

However, being dependent in your partnership can create problems. There have been many books written about co-dependency as a condition to be corrected. Ms. Ford says, "Your soulmate is not there to fix you or change you."

I once worked with a woman who told her husband, "You are the sun; I am the moon; and my life revolves around you." As you might imagine, the person hearing that might experience his need for freedom kick in. This man did. He had a series of affairs and eventually divorced his "moon."

Having your partner confess that her life is totally dependent on you creates an awesome responsibility and burden. It is difficult enough being responsible for yourself and for any dependent children. An unnecessary layer of responsibility is added when you must also be responsible for another grown, capable adult.

Couples who fall far into the dependence end of the continuum can be similar to addicts needing crack. When they get their "partner fix" they feel high. But without their partner's constant attention, they are so low. A woman once told me that she couldn't be happy when her boyfriend was unhappy. That's dependence. Your mood does not have to be linked inseparably to your partner's. You are two different people.

There are some people who clearly want to feel needed in a relationship. This need is usually manifested as a high level of nurturing or protection. If this is your pattern you may actually welcome, and even encourage, some degree of dependence in your partner.

People with a high need for love and belonging generally want to be needed. It helps them to feel loved. They can actually encourage dependence in their partner in order to get their own needs met. Dependent people in relationships may also be getting their needs met by relying on their partner exclusively for love and problem solving. The dependent person does not want conflict and attempts to become the person her partner wants, whether or not it is who she actually is. Dependent people may stay in the relationship longer than is healthy because they believe they hold the key to making the relationship work.

Similarly, people with a high security need often want to ensure that the people they care about are secure. They want to protect their loved ones unconditionally. People in this situation can also encourage their partner to be dependent so it's easier for them to provide protection. They may stay in the relationship longer than is healthy because the protectors don't believe their partner can survive without them and the people being protected believe this assertion.

Independence

From the time you turned two years-old, you began to push for more independence from your parents. You wanted to do things yourself and explore your world. This process continues and grows in scope until adolescence and into young adulthood, when you separate from your parents.

This is the best time to reach your personal pinnacle of independence. You want to know that you are capable of taking care of yourself financially, physically, and emotionally. You want to know that if you don't know how to do something, you can at least access the resources to get it done.

Some people can carry independence to an extreme, particularly if they have a high need for freedom. Their mantra becomes, "If I want something done right, I have to do it myself." They have great difficulty admitting that they need help, let alone actually asking for it. People with a high degree of independence can end relationships quickly. They don't like to deal with the compromises sometimes needed in relationships.

People who have experienced pain from previous relationships may be cautious, which results in an independent attitude. They may also have a fear of commitment—a fear that this may not be the "right" partner for the long haul. Another explanation for the extreme independent position is the fear of losing oneself. People think that if they allow interdependence with another, then they may lose who they are individually because they will merge with their partner.

Fear is generally the cause of an extreme independent position. You may protect yourself in this manner but you won't be able to experience the true value of a healthy, interdependent relationship.

The key in relationships is to find the optimal balance for you as a couple, adjusting this balance as your relationship goes through different relationship seasons.

Interdependence

In the research, 23% of the happy couples surveyed mentioned interdependence as an ingredient that made their relationship work. They responded that time together was critical but so was time apart. They needed the freedom to be individuals, separate from their relationship.

Once people achieve a state of independence, they feel safe in the knowledge that, if necessary, they can make it alone. Some will choose to stay independent for life. However those who wish to engage in a committed relationship will find that the right degree of interdependence seems to be most healthy for the relationship.

Interdependence can take many forms. Sometimes couples divide up household chores and each person is responsible for his or her own. Sometimes certain activities are understood to always be done together. Couples may choose to combine finances to create interdependence. Others have interdependence in parenting. There may also be interdependence in problem-solving and decision-making, where major decisions are made together. Whatever form the interdependence takes is determined by the needs and desires of the couple.

In an interdependent relationship, couples do many things together and they also engage in activities apart. There is support for the freedom to do things alone or with other people, as long as their relationship remains of primary importance.

Ms. Ford asks the question, "If you want somebody else to make you feel good, what can you do to make them feel good?" That is a question of interdependence.

Shawn and Danielle

I had the honor and pleasure of being at their wedding ten years ago. This couple had a very healthy balance of interdependence based on their particular needs. Both Shawn and Danielle have high needs for freedom. They both waited until their 30s to marry as they had some trepidation about finding a partner who would allow the freedom they each needed.

Shawn is an artist and Danielle an actor/director. Both are highly cre-

ative and were able to generate just enough income to support themselves with some occasional help from their parents.

When they decided to get married, I was pleasantly surprised that they were able to give each other the independence they needed to survive as individuals. This in turn nurtured their relationship and made it stronger. After mastering maintaining their individual independence within their relationship, they grew into interdependence.

They bought a house together, pooling finances, and created a home. They waited eight years and then had a baby. They are very interdependent in their parenting. They consult each other and confer on almost every decision about their child. When they engage in activities together, usually centered around family time, they are very attentive to each other, while allowing room for each of them to have alone time with extended family members, if desired.

This is not a pattern of interdependence that would work for all couples but it is the perfect pattern for Shawn and Danielle. It's closer to the independent end of the continuum but this is what they need as a couple and as individuals to survive. They have found their perfect balance for this time of their lives.

The Balance

On the Dependence/Interdependence/Independence Continuum, successful couples find the optimum balance needed for their relationship, which is the key to success. This balance can be achieved though trial and error or by deliberate negotiation. It generally involves balancing the love and belonging need with the freedom need.

If you both have a high need for love and belonging, then your balance will be more toward the dependent end. If you both have a high need for freedom then your balance will be closer to the independent end.

Relationships where one partner has a high need for freedom and the other has a high need for love and belonging can be challenging. The people with the higher love and belonging need will not understand their partner's need for independence and separation, since that is relatively foreign to them. The people with the high freedom need will have difficulty understanding their partner's need for closeness and togetherness, because they don't share that same desire.

Another step in maintaining this precarious balance is to check in with each other on a regular basis to determine where each of you stands. Openness and effective communication are critical in establishing and maintaining this important interdependent balance. What may work on Monday, may not achieve the proper balance on Saturday. Circumstances change and individual's needs change.

Questions to Consider

1. Where do you fall on the Dependence/Interdependence/Independence Continuum in your relationship with your partner?

2. Where do you each want to be?

3. What steps can you take toward finding your couple's perfect balance?

4. What's one thing you are willing to do this week to attain a more optimal balance for your relationship?

Balance is never perfected . . . it waxes and wanes . . . ebbs and flows. Couples who know how to be flexible with the adjustments tend to do much better. In conversation with your partner, be up front about how you are feeling, and discuss what can be done to achieve or maintain your relationship's balance. Working together with your partner, find, create, and maintain the optimal balance of interdependence for your relationship at any given point in time.

We will talk more about this in the chapters on Appreciating Differences and Negotiating for the Win/Win/Win. For now what you need to know is:

1. As a couple it is important to find the balance.

2. Each of you is committed to finding that balance.

3. While seeking that balance, you are willing to prioritize your relationship needs over what each of you wants as an individual. You move from the dependence or the independence ends of the continuum toward the interdependent center position.

4. Know that this is constant process.

This process will enable you to move from either end of the Continuum toward the Interdependent center position.

Problem Identification

Much tension is created for couples because they inaccurately define who owns a certain problem in their relationship. When people are unhappy about what their partners are doing, instead of owning the problem because they are the ones upset, they declare that their partners have the problem and set about getting them to solve it.

When you are the one most upset by a situation, understand that your emotional involvement in it makes *you* the one with the problem. From an interdependent position, you would explain to your partner what it is you don't like and request him or her to adjust so that your problem can be solved. Sometimes this approach will be successful. Suppose your wife loves to blast music you don't like while cleaning the house. You let her know and she agrees to wear headphones. This is an interdependent solution.

But what happens if you ask your wife to change and she doesn't cooperate? Does this mean that she doesn't love you? Of course not, it simply means that whatever is a problem for you isn't high on her agenda and may not even be within her conscious awareness.

A Benefit of Interdependence

Because the nature of a committed relationship is interdependence, you can affect a positive change in your relationship without your partner's conscious cooperation.

Let's say Patty wants Jason to turn the heat down before he comes to bed at night. She's asked repeatedly but Jason just doesn't remember to do it. Patty can move to the dependent end of the Continuum, insisting that she cannot be happy unless Jason remembers to turn the heat down. In that case she is putting her contentment totally in Jason's hands. That's the definition of dependence.

However, Patty could recognize that *she* is the one who wants the heat down at night. Jason isn't opposed to having the heat lowered; he just doesn't remember to do it. So Patty could move to a more independent position and recognize that this is her problem not Jason's. She can begin to turn the heat down when she goes to bed. She has fixed her problem. This will also create positive change in their relationship because Patty will stop nagging Jason about the heat and will no longer be angry with him for not complying with her request.

I often work with individuals who are not happy in their relationship but their partner does not want to come for counseling. Many therapists may take this as a sign that the partner is not committed to the relationship. I approach this scenario from a different angle.

Since the only person's behavior you can control is your own, I find it very useful to ascertain what you can do to make the relationship better without expecting anything in return. What predictably happens due to interdependence is when one person changes, the other person changes too and the relationship improves.

Back to Independence

It is highly likely that, regardless of your relationship, at some point you will need to be independent again. Your relationship could end. One of you may become physically dependent on the other. And it's possible your partner could die, leaving you alone again. We'll discuss this grieving phase of relationships in chapter 18. But for now, be reassured that if you find yourself alone, you are capable of achieving independence again.

Chapter Eight Summary

1. We begin our lives as dependent and then move into independence.

2. When we choose to enter a committed relationship, it is best to move to an interdependent position.

3. Finding the optimal balance on the Dependence/Interdependence/Independence Continuum is a relationship task for you and your partner to negotiate together based on your individual and relationship needs.

4. Ask for what you want. But if you don't get it, take responsibility for the solution, temporarily moving toward independence to correct *your* problem.

5. It's possible to improve your relationship by making changes yourself.

6. Being able to return to independence is critical to your success if or when your relationship ends.

Jealousy

A Deadly Relationship Killer

Life is either a daring adventure or nothing.
Security does not exist in nature, nor do the
children of men as a whole experience it.
Avoiding danger is no safer in the long run than exposure.

—Helen Keller

Jealousy is a definite killer in a relationship. It is the exact opposite of trust, which will be discussed further in chapter 13.

There are basically four roots of jealousy:

1. Insecurity
2. Past experiences
3. Viewing your partner as a possession
4. A strong belief things should never change

Let's examine each of these separately.

Insecurity

Jealousy is a natural response when you are unsure of who you are or don't like yourself. You don't believe that you deserve your current relationship. You believe that you are fundamentally flawed somehow so how could anyone want only you? If this describes you, you will have a difficult time whenever your partner is around potential sexual partners. Your insecurity will cause you to imagine that your partner is engaging in all kinds of sexual encounters. As long as you believe your partner is unfaithful, whether true or not, you will not have a healthy, satisfied, happy relationship.

You will need to spend some time in chapter 2 figuring out who you are and what value you bring to a relationship. You will need to begin to appreciate the unique gift you are and believe that others can see it too.

Past Experiences

Almost everyone has had the experience of someone they cared for lying to them or cheating on them. When this happens a person's natural inclination is to ask the question, "What's wrong with me?" It's taken personally. The "victim" begins to wonder, "What did I do to deserve this? Why didn't I recognize this from the beginning?"

When you doubt yourself, you tend to erect walls around your heart to protect yourself from pain, either real or anticipated. Your current partner has done nothing to earn your mistrust but you are carrying baggage from past relationships and punishing him or her unfairly.

If this is your pattern, please pay attention to chapter 13, which outlines how to learn to trust again. You must stop taking past incidents personally and move forward courageously. To play it safe means a life without true, unconditional love. While it may be safer, is this the kind of life you want?

Viewing Your Partner as a Possession

Once you commit to each other in a relationship, sometimes one or both partners start to view their significant other as a possession. You begin to call each other "*my* man," "*my* woman," "*my* husband" or "*my* wife." You expect certain behaviors of the person who "belongs" to you. You want your partner to behave exactly as you expect—and that does not include any flirtation or involvement with potential sexual partners.

People who view their partner as a possession feel perfectly justified dictating their partner's behavior. I remember a boyfriend in college telling me, "No girlfriend of mine will ride horses or be on the equestrian team," right after I had attended an equestrian team meeting. Needless to say, he wasn't my boyfriend after that!

If it is your pattern to view your partner as your possession, then you need to begin viewing him or her as a separate entity with hopes and desires that may differ from yours. Your partner may, at times, engage in behavior of which you do not approve.

If you try to hold water tightly in your hand, it will flow out between your fingers. But if you cup your hand without trying to prevent the water's flow, it will stay in your open palm. This is how relationships work as well.

I remember a quote from Richard Bach who said, "If you love someone, set them free. If they come back they're yours; if they don't, they never were." Treat your relationship this way. When you stop trying to possess your partner, he or she will be more likely to stay. If he or she leaves, then your partner wasn't the right one for you, or perhaps it wasn't the right time.

A Strong Belief Things Should Never Change

As the Helen Keller quote at the beginning of this chapter states, there are no guarantees in life. Someone may love you with all they have and later leave you for someone else. You can seek promises and actually get them, leading to three possible outcomes: fulfillment, broken promises, or someone staying with you out of guilt or obligation. Would you want your partner to stay with you out of a sense of duty when his or her heart longed to be elsewhere? Likely not.

If you tend to expect things to never change and look for assurances of forever, stop! Do your absolute best to live in the moment. Have your motto be, "for today, for this moment." When you release yourself and your partner from forever promises, what you often get is forever. And if you don't, you aren't devastated. You recognize the transience of relationships and you appreciate the time you had. You accept that some relationships end. You take the time to regroup, as discussed in chapter 2 and you prepare for the next stage in your life.

To Tell or Not to Tell

People in relationships where jealousy abounds often play mind games. They are capable of setting up scenarios to purposely create jealousy in their partner. Some people think that if their partners aren't jealous, then they don't care. So they may flirt to elicit jealousy.

In other situations, your partner may make inquiries into another person's interest in you—innocent or outright disrespectful. How should you handle these questions? Do you answer them or keep the information to yourself? Whatever your answer, what is your motivation? In my experience, there are differences among individuals in this area.

I have informally surveyed men and women on this subject and a pattern has emerged. Most women said they would respond to these inquiries, in order to be open and honest with their partner. They didn't want their partner to find out something innocent and jump to the wrong conclusion. They worried that if their partners heard anything through the grapevine, and they hadn't told them, then the partners would jump to the conclusion they had something to hide. Not surprisingly, most women believe that their partner is hiding something if he has been silent on the subject.

On the other hand, men tend not to tell. Their thinking tends to be, if nothing happened, then there is nothing to tell. They are not interested in starting problems where none exist. They fear that if they tell their partner, she will become jealous and start asking a lot of questions, thus creating unnecessary stress on the relationship. When a woman tells a man about her innocent encounters, he generally does not appreciate her for being forthcoming. He tends to think that she is attempting to make him jealous.

This is not to say that there aren't exceptions. You may be in a relationship where you both share the same opinions about what to tell and your motivation for doing so. However, in most relationships, men are behaving in the way they wished their partner would behave; and women are doing the same. This is following the antiquated Golden Rule of doing unto others as you would have them do unto you. As discussed previously, in intimate relationships it is far better to use the Platinum Rule of doing unto others as *they* would have you do unto them.

In the spirit of the Platinum Rule, it is important to ask your partner about his or her preference, if a situation exists where someone is interested in you. Does he or she want to know or not? Talk about it before a problem exists and give them what they tell you they want—not what you would want in a similar situation.

Being Present in the Now

If you are someone prone to jealousy, your best strategy is to stay present in the moment. If you need further instruction on how to do this, read Eckhart Tolle's book, *The Power of Now*. In it, Tolle expands on how there are no problems in the now.

Whenever you find yourself obsessing about what may or may not have happened in the past, bring your conscious attention back to what you are doing in the moment. Similarly, if you are worrying about what might be happening in the future, reorient yourself to the present moment.

When engaging in either past or future thoughts, we are completely missing what is happening right now. What if this moment is all we have? What if something totally unexpected takes us from our life as we know it? Do we want to spend our last moment regretting the past or worrying about the future?

Shouldn't we offer our partner our best in the moment? If you stay fully present to the moment, there will be no room for jealousy, nagging about things not done, worrying about bills not paid, preoccupation with work, worry about children, and any host of over things.

Be present in each moment, but especially be present when you are with the ones you love. They deserve your complete attention and appreciation for the moment being shared.

Brian and Amy

Brian and Amy are a couple who are often separated because she travels a lot for work. She recognized she was not staying present in the moment whenever she was getting ready to leave town. She was often conflicted about leaving. She loved her job but she always missed Brian while she was away. Usually two or three days before she was to leave, she would become quiet and sad, already missing him before she left. One day, Brian asked her what was wrong and Amy replied, "I miss you." Brian responded with, "I'm right here." This answer helped Amy realize that she was wasting the beautiful moments she did have with Brian anticipating the time they would be separated. After that, whenever she began to feel sad about going, she redirected her thoughts to the present moment and felt grateful for the great relationship they have and the time they do have together.

The Upper Limit Problem

Author Dr. Gay Hendricks writes about the Upper Limit Problem in his groundbreaking book, *The Big Leap*. He says that people can only tolerate so much success in certain areas. Once they reach their limit of success, they tend to sabotage themselves from exceeding the level of success that's comfortable for them.

Marci Shimoff in her book, *Happy for No Reason*, also discusses a happiness set point. She writes that people have a set point for how much happiness they can stand. When things are going better than they think they deserve, people tend to engage in unconscious self-sabotage. Sometimes this takes the form of jealousy.

Has this ever happened to you? Your relationship was sailing along and everything was great. You may have been going through a particularly intimate time where you were feeling closer than ever to your partner and you did something to mess it up. Perhaps you accused your partner of being unfaithful. Or you may have even entertained or engaged in an affair. Why does this happen?

Matthew and Carol

Matthew and Carol were at about the six-month mark in their relationship and everything was going very well. Carol was one of my coaching clients and we had been working on recognizing the upper limits she experiences in her finances, her weight, and her relationships.

She and Matthew had gone away for a weekend and were having a wonderful time. Matthew left Carol for a brief time to go the store. As she was basking in the memory of the wonderful time they had been having, an unwelcome thought popped into her head. She thought, I wonder why Matthew hasn't introduced me to his mother yet? He must not be as serious about me as I think he is.

Because of her conscious attention, she was able to recognize that thought as self-sabotage and switch it to something more helpful. In Carol's case, she didn't grill and attack Matthew upon his return. Amazingly, the very next day, Matthew proposed that he and Carol go to his mother's house to play cards in the near future.

Keeping a vigilant eye out for your own self-sabotage can greatly enhance your relationships.

For a more thorough explanation, read Gay Hendricks' book *The Big Leap.* You need to uncover the old childhood messages that tell you that you don't deserve to be happier than whatever your set point is. Take these subconscious messages from the dark and bring them into the light where you can examine them for truth. What you typically find is that they have no basis in fact or reality at all. As you come to understand that there is no limit to your happiness or success in any area of your life, you can cease the self-sabotage and raise your set point using affirmations that honor your value and worth.

You will gradually be able to tolerate longer and better periods of intimacy and love in your relationship. Won't that be great!

Chapter Nine Summary

1. Jealousy stems from four roots: insecurity, past experiences, viewing your partner as a possession, and expecting things to never change.

2. You can take steps to move yourself away from jealous behavior.

3. Men and women have differences concerning whether they want to know about certain issues. Find out what your partner prefers and give it to him or her.

4. Staying present in the moment will help you overcome jealous behavior.

5. Overcoming your Upper Limit Problem in relationships will assist you to stop sabotaging your relationship with jealous behavior.

Sex and Romance
The Dance Begins

*The main problem in marriage is that for a man sex is
a hunger like eating. If the man is hungry and can't get to
a fancy French restaurant, he goes to a hot dog stand.
For a woman, what is important is love and romance.*

—Joan Fontaine

Partners often have differences in the areas of sex and romance. In my research, 15% of those interviewed complained of wanting more or less intimacy in their relationships—and these are couples who report being happy and satisfied! Fifty-six percent of respondents didn't mention sex at all as a positive or negative factor in their relationship; while 29% reported great sex as an important component in the success of their relationship. Nineteen percent of couples in my research spoke of romance and physical touch, i.e., holding hands, cuddling, and massage—as being important in their relationship. Eight-one percent did not mention it. Compatibility in this area appears to be a challenge. Early in the relationship, couples may begin as sexually compatible but end up in different places as time goes on.

The Dance

In Don Miguel Ruiz' book, *The Mastery of Love,* he describes how people play roles with each other, making it impossible to know with whom you are actually in relationship.

> *When a man meets a woman, he makes an image of her from his point of view, and the woman makes an image of the man from her point of view. Then he tries to make her fit the image he makes for her, and she tries to make him fit the image she makes for him. Now there are six images between them. Of course they are lying to each other, even if they don't know they are lying. Their relationship is based on fear, it is based on lies. It is not based on truth, because they cannot see through all that fog.*

Ruiz' point is that because of our early childhood messages and programming, none of us really know who we are. Then when we get into relationships with other people, we tend to act out the role we think we are supposed to play with that person, and things get really interesting from there!

I blame Disney, and other forms of media, as major contributors to the fact that couples seem to be less compatible in the sex and romance department.

Women: From the time little girls are old enough to watch a movie, they are bombarded with the message: The love of a good woman will save any "bad" man. Girls are exposed to this message very early, as in the message in *Beauty and the Beast.* Add to this the stereotype of the romantic Prince Charming who sweeps women off their feet, and is it any wonder girls grow up expecting perfection, both from themselves and their partners? And of course, as girls mature into women, these messages abound in soap operas, weekly television series, and big screen movies. We actually come to believe in a perfect partner and relationship, at least subconsciously.

As a woman begins to date, she seeks the raw material of a Prince Charming. She knows she will not find him in true prince form; he will have to be molded and created by her. When a potential mate presents himself and meets her approval, she often reinvents herself so she will appear to be the perfect life partner for whom he searches.

Once the woman determines this man to have the raw material with which she can work, she may make him wait but will eventually offer herself to him sexually. Typically, after their initial encounter, the couple engages in frequent, exuberant, adventurous sex. In the beginning, he is trying to be her prince. He wants to please her. She understands how much he values their physical relationship and wants to give him that. Since she is always the attentive, willing, even eager sexual partner, he begins to believe he has found the woman of his dreams.

Men: Men are fairly simple. They are visual beings and thus look for a partner who is physically attractive to them. A man generally wants freedom to be his own man, while experiencing peace in his relationship.

He is happy to have a woman who is sexually responsive and non-demanding in their relationship. Since she is working hard to impress him, it is easy for him to be impressed. He recognizes that the woman in his life needs more verbal communication and romance. He may not understand why but as long as she is expressing her love physically, he is willing to express his emotionally.

Women generally need romance as foreplay to sexual activity. While the occasional cave man conquering scenario can be very satisfying, as a general rule women want to know that their man really knows their deepest desires and wants to prove his love through patience and romance.

For a woman, sexual activity begins long before the bedroom. It's about non-sexual touching, sharing feelings, and special appreciation. A love note in the morning could set the stage for a sexual encounter that evening. Cooking for your woman, dancing with her in your living room, giving her a foot rub, brushing her hair, talking and listening to each other with interest about your respective days, can all be foreplay for great sex later.

The Problem

While it is difficult to determine where it actually starts, something gradually and insidiously changes in the relationship.

Many men make the decision to marry a woman believing they will have 24-hour access to a willing and exciting sexual partner. When this promise is left unfulfilled, they feel cheated and lose their desire to romance their partner.

Whether it is that the man is not cooperating with the woman's "molding" process, or he figures he has won the woman so he no longer needs to pursue her romantically, the relationship begins to be less pleasing.

As their sexual and/or romantic needs are not being met as well as they used to be, they begin giving each other less and less of what the other desires. Women become less sexual and men become less romantic.

When a man is feeling criticized and disrespected, the last thing he has on his mind is romance. He will still be interested in the act of intercourse but he has lost the inspiration for romance.

When a woman is approached by a man for sex without romance, she is less inclined to oblige. At that point, sex begins to feel like a job—one more thing on her "to do list" before she can go to sleep. If she does engage in sex, it is usually without a willing spirit which causes the man to feel underappreciated and disrespected even more.

When partners begin withdrawing from each other, they tend to withdraw the thing their partner needs the most. Women will withdraw sex and men will withdraw attention. Complaining, blaming, and criticizing move into the relationship. This does not bode well for the future of their intimate life together.

Relationship expert Dr. Dennis Neder writes about how partners are willing to speak their partner's language but will revert to their own when feeling neglected, unloved, or disrespected.

Areas of Harmony, Tension, or Conflict

When couples are locked into the withdrawal cycle described above, there is great conflict about their sexual/intimacy needs. They believe that their partners don't accept, understand, respect, and love them. There may be conflict in terms of arguing and fighting about these differences or there may be tension, which is what occurs whenever the topic of intimacy is not discussed. The feelings of rejection, abandonment, and criticism are still there but aren't being talked about.

Even healthier intimate relationships, where the withdrawing cycle has not begun, experience many areas of potential conflict.

Exclusivity can be an area of conflict, more often in the beginning of a relationship. It is unusual for both people in a relationship to be ready for exclusivity at precisely the same time. Neder says, "In my experience, while women want/need it, it's more commonly a point of tolerance to men."

Many relationships are strained when one partner pressures the other for exclusivity before that person is ready.

If you want exclusivity in your relationship but your partner is not ready, allow your partner to be where he or she is. If you are not happy with this arrangement, then you have four options available to you:

1. You can threaten or give ultimatums to your partner, hoping he or she will commit.

2. You can quietly suffer, wishing things were different.

3. You can decide to accept where your partner is and wait to see if he or she grows into the desire for exclusivity.

4. You can decide exclusivity is a non-negotiable for you and end the relationship.

I would recommend deep soul-searching to determine if your partner is more important than exclusivity or if exclusivity is the most important thing to you. I don't advise threatening or bribing your partner into exclusivity. It could end your relationship or you could end up with a less than heartfelt commitment you will likely regret later.

Other areas that can lead to tension or conflict are frequency and duration of sexual activity. I once spoke with a couple where the husband expected sex twice daily at scheduled times. His wife was not opposed to having sex twice daily but wanted some flexibility on the time schedule. He would become frustrated if she didn't have sex at precisely the designated time. They decided to divorce.

Some couples enjoy more frequent sex when they are younger, but find that their sex drive decreases as they age or they experience some physical challenges. This only becomes an area of tension or conflict if both partners are not experiencing the same declining interest in sexual activity.

Sam

One man who took my survey explained, "I wanted sex more than she did. I overcame it by volunteering for two tours of duty in Southeast Asia. She was ready for sex each time we met during and after those tours." I don't think you have to sign up for an overseas military tour of duty in order to generate intimacy in your relationship. You just need to focus on giving your partner the things he or she wants and needs most. Unless there is unresolved psychological trauma, you should be able to create more desire in your relationship.

Another area of conflict or tension may be the duration of sexual activity. Some people like to engage in sexual activity for longer periods of time than others. Sometimes the amount of foreplay desired is different for each partner.

Variety is something that can create conflict. One partner may be perfectly happy and satisfied to engage in sexual activity in a similar way every time while the other partner may want to try variations on the theme.

Some partners like to plan their intimacy like a date, while others prefer the freedom and fun of a spontaneous sexual encounter.

Another area of potential conflict I see in couples is the time of day that the sexual activity occurs. Some people prefer having sex at night, while others prefer morning. Still others have no preference, any time will do! This only becomes a conflict when one partner is always trying to insist on things being his or her way.

When striving for harmony, it's important to know yourself and know your partner. You must be clear about what you like, what you are willing to do but aren't necessarily crazy about, and what you absolutely don't like and don't want to do. Try to keep items in this last category to a minimum. A sense of exploration and a willingness to try new things is healthy in a committed, loving relationship.

Knowing your partner is about listening to your partner's likes and dislikes—exploring their sexual fantasies, and developing a willing spirit to do things that are particularly pleasing to your partner, without compromising on the things you are unwilling to do. While you should not compromise your morals or integrity, pleasing your partner in this area is incredibly important, particularly if you are in a monogamous relationship. You are the only outlet your partner has for creating a satisfying, intimate, sexual experience.

If satisfying your partner more sexually is an area you are invested in, then I would highly recommend Dr. Kevin Leman's book, *Sheet Music*.

Satisfying Each Other's Needs:
People engaging in romance and sex can experience it physically, mentally, emotionally, spiritually or in any combination thereof. If you tend to experience sex spiritually and your partner tends to experience sex more physically, this will not be a problem unless you have the need for similar experiences and insist that your partner use your primary mode of sexual experience.

When you are able to allow each other to experience intimacy in the way that is best for each of you, then you will be in harmony. Spend time finding out what type of experiences your partner enjoys. Listen to him or her, believing what your partner says.

Once you know what experiences carry the most value for your partner, be sure to provide these experiences for each other. Do not insist that your partner value the same experiences you do. Simply honor each other's needs as being different and know each of you can be satisfied.

When it comes to sex and romance, it does not have to be an either/ or experience. It is not only possible, but highly advisable, to create an "and" situation, where you AND your partner can both be satisfied.

Pete and Linda

For several years early in their relationship, Pete was dissatisfied because it was important to him for Linda to have an orgasm during intercourse. It wasn't until Pete accepted the fact that the physical component of sex was not as valuable to Linda as the spiritual experience, that he became satisfied with their sex life.

Enjoying what you enjoy while creating opportunities for your partner to enjoy what is important to him or her is the way to find harmony. Again it's the Platinum Rule in action.

Sex and romance can be the most beautiful thing in a committed, loving relationship. It requires each partner to be willing to listen and explore different things while remaining true to their own limitations.

If you are interested in explicit help in this area, Krisanna Jeffery has created explicit exercises where couples have a structured way of addressing and correcting sexual challenges in a positive, non-threatening, and empowering way. To explore her work, visit www.GreatSexForLifeToolkit.com.

Chapter Ten Summary

1. Couple's often begin their relationship with an abundance of sex and romance only to discover, after committing to a long-term relationship, that this early receptivity is replaced by indifference.

2. Women tend to require more romance prior to lovemaking. Men are more interested in the actual act of intercourse.

3. During times of disharmony in the relationship, women tend to withdraw sex, while men tend to withdraw romance.

4. There are many areas that can create conflict in the sexuality area. Working through these differences will strengthen your relationship and provide a place of comfort, relaxation, and care for both of you.

Effective Communication

Increasing the Odds You Will Be Heard

Success in marriage does not come merely through
finding the right mate, but through being the right mate.

–Barnett Brickner

Everybody knows how important communication is in a relationship, right? Not necessarily. Some people are introverted and don't like much talking and verbal processing in their relationship. Other people value communication very highly. In every relationship, there are communication challenges to be overcome simply because two different people come from two different backgrounds and hence communicate differently.

It's important that you do your best to understand and honor your partner's uniqueness and communication preferences. If you have a partner who is a person of few words, then find other, nonverbal ways to communicate. You may be able to communicate deep caring to your loved one simply through companionship, which is its own form of communication.

If you are generally a quiet person but your partner needs to keep talking about things, and you believe you've heard her several times saying exactly the same thing, honor her enough to listen one more time. Relationship expert Betsy Sansby says, "Women complain that men are clueless and men complain that women are never satisfied. The problem is that women think they're being clear when they're really not, and men assume they understand when they really don't." She suggests that men can "assume that his partner wouldn't be repeating herself if she really felt heard." Ask her to say it in a different way so you're sure you really understand.

While some communication differences have been attributed to gender differences, others are due to personality differences, some to environment and culture, and still others to genetic influences. The cause is unimportant unless it helps you determine what to do about it. Let's take a closer look at some common communication challenges and how to overcome them.

Communication Differences

Many documented differences between men and women's needs, desires, and communication styles have been attributed to gender. Dr. John Gray wrote *Men are from Mars; Women are from Venus* to highlight some of these differences.

I will reiterate some of Dr. Gray's findings while adding some of my own. However I don't want you to get the impression that these are absolutes. There are always exceptions to the rules but in general, there are some traits belonging almost exclusively to males and others belonging exclusively to females. Should you or your partner fall into the exception category, do not be concerned. It simply means you don't follow the typical pattern.

The main communication differences between men and women are in the following areas:
1. Internal vs. External Processing
2. Being Intellectual vs. Emotional
3. Needing Respect vs. Love
4. Communicating Directly vs. Indirectly
5. After Commitment: Ending Courtship vs. Improvement Plan
6. Apologies: Doing Penance vs. Saying "I'm Sorry"
7. Compartmentalizing vs. Not
8. Parenting Your Partner

9. Different Timing

10. When Angry: Shutting Down vs. Using Absolutes

11. Optimism vs. Pessimism (not gender related)

Let's examine these in some detail.

Internal vs. External Processing

Let's begin with daily problem-solving. Men process internally, while women process externally. For example, men prefer solitude when attempting to solve their problems. Women tend to problem-solve by discussing the events with those close to them.

When a woman attempts to process with her male counterpart, he is likely to assume one of two things: a) She wants him to fix the "problem" or b) She is looking for advice. Most women are not seeking either of the above. They are simply looking for understanding and support. This scenario often creates frustration for both males and females, as neither is getting what they want from the exchange.

When a man is upset, his woman generally works hard to get him to talk to her. She wants to know what's wrong so she can listen and support him. From his point of view, however, it seems that his woman is nagging him and trying to get him to talk when he needs his space. The woman, on the other hand, is wondering what she did wrong that he won't even talk to her.

When a woman is upset, her man predictably will either leave her alone to give her space or offer unsolicited advice. From her point of view it seems that her man either won't listen or doesn't understand that she isn't looking for solutions. Men are thinking at this point, *How many times am I going to have to listen to this story!* Or, *If you only do what I suggested, it would all work out.*

When women are upset, men need to listen to them without offering advice—just listen to their story and empathize with their feelings. Women need to seek a female friend with whom to vent, rather than expecting their man to listen without attempting to escape or fix things.

When men are upset, women need to respect that they need space to work out their problems. They need to understand that men's silence does not mean that something is wrong with their relationship. It most likely has nothing to do with them. Men need to explain that they need space—that they aren't angry with their partner and that they will be back.

Being Intellectual vs. Emotional

Women tend to express a wide range of emotions, while men tend to be more logical and intellectual about their relationship. As a result, men may consider their partners to be overly emotional and irrational. "That time of the month" is sometimes used by men to explain their partner's moods. This, in turn, can infuriate women because they feel that their partner is uncaring and cold. Women want their men to display some passion but men tend to respond with their intellect.

Both intellectual and emotional approaches are helpful in problem solving. However we tend to be self-righteous believing that our way is the best way. Men who tend to solve their problems intellectually, probably don't value those who process emotionally, and vice versa. It is important to see that both approaches have value and can provide a healthy balance in relationships.

Men, you need to stay and support your woman when she is emotional. Do not run from the situation. Know that she is not looking for solutions, but for understanding. Women, stop insisting that your partner always share his feelings with you. That's your need, not his!

Needing Respect vs. Love

When partners communicate with each other, they often give their partner what they, themselves, value most. Dr. Emerson Eggerichs wrote a book about this very issue entitled, *Love & Respect.* His premise is that women most value love from their mate, while men are seeking respect.

Dr. Eggerichs proposes that the main problem between couples who are not getting along is that the men are not being loving enough toward their wives, and the wives are being too critical and disrespectful of their husbands. Women need unconditional love from their man; men need unconditional respect from their woman.

He further goes on to state that these two factors have an interactive effect. When a woman isn't feeling loved by her man, she will become more critical and withdraw her respect. Similarly, when a man isn't feeling respected by his woman, he will withdraw his love. So you can see that this can be a vicious downward cycle. As men become less loving, their women show less respect. As women show less respect, their men become less loving. It's difficult to pinpoint how it starts but the author calls this the "crazy cycle."

It is important to remember that this crazy cycle exists when communicating with your partner. Women, you want to use language that communicates appreciation and respect to your partner. Men, you want to use language that allows your partner to know how much you love and cherish her.

Communicating Directly vs. Indirectly

Another area where men are different from women involves how direct they are in communicating. Most men will say what they mean and are fairly straight forward about it. Women, who are so adept at tuning in to emotions, tend to look for the meaning behind the words. But with men, there usually isn't any hidden meaning; what they say is what they mean.

Women, on the other hand, tend to be less direct in their communication relying on their partner's mind reading abilities to simply "know" what it is they want. I'll let you in on a secret . . . Men are *not* mind readers! Women, you need to let your partner know exactly what you want. Never mind what the fairy tales tell you; men do not magically know what you want. Regardless of how much he loves you, he needs you to tell him directly what you want.

Men, take the time to ask and really listen to what your partner wants. When she does risk telling you, if it is possible and reasonable, try to give it to her. This will increase the likelihood that she will be direct with you in the future, rather than withdrawing when you can't successfully read her mind.

After Commitment: Ending Courtship vs. Improvement Plan

Have you ever heard that old adage that says, "Men marry women hoping they will never change, and women marry men hoping they will"? This speaks to another fundamental difference between men and women, which we discussed in detail in the chapter on sex and romance. After committing, women try to improve their men, and the men stop being romantic, the way they were when they dated. At some point the woman has to realize that the man isn't going along with the improvement program she has for him.

Women, you need to stop trying to change your men! Appreciate the man he is right now. If he wasn't the man you wanted before you committed to him, the odds are that he still won't be the man you want after you are committed. Men, continue your courtship even after she's committed to you. Continue to create romance in your relationship. This will increase the odds that she won't change and will continue to shower you with the love and affection you desire.

Apologies: Doing Penance vs. Saying "I'm Sorry"

Men tend to think that apologizing shows some form of weakness, whereas women feel that an apology makes everything all right.

Men, you do not have to admit blame to apologize for hurting your partner, whether intentionally or unintentionally. You can say that you are sorry she is hurting. Women, know that your man will be looking for more than an apology if you did him wrong. Be prepared to do penance with a behavior change. A simple, "I'm sorry" just won't cut it.

Compartmentalizing vs. Not

Another difference between men and women is the ability, or lack thereof, to compartmentalize. Many men have the ability to compartmentalize. This means that they can deal with something swiftly, put it in its place, and move on. Women often lack this ability; there is frequently carry over from one thing to the next. As a result, women have often been labeled as "moody," when in actuality they are still upset about something that happened earlier that their partner has already forgotten.

This difference in compartmentalization is due to different wiring of the male and female brains. Simply understanding this difference without judging it can make your communications smoother.

Parenting Your Partner

Have you ever heard verbal exchanges between men and women were embarrassingly similar to the way parents talk to their misbehaving children? Because the main relationships we have experienced in our lives were with our primary caregivers, sometimes we fall into patterns of acting like bad parents with our life partners. This is not appropriate.

Scolding, reprimanding, and punishing are forms of communication this approach can take. Men may yell at their women or punish them by withdrawing into silence. Women may nag their men or scold them as if they were children. Our significant others are not our children and should not be treated as such.

Missy and Dan

Missy and Dan are married. He is a man who likes to gamble and Missy treats him like a child. She scolds him and has him on an allowance. She makes him bring her receipts for his expenses and checks up on him all the time. I'm not saying Dan is always honest or that he doesn't have challenges of his own. But when Missy treats him as if she is his mother, then he only gets better at lying to avoid her detection. I suspect that he gambles even more than he would if she treated him more like an equal partner. It creates a huge strain on their marriage and you can believe he doesn't really hear much of what she has to say.

In loving, adult relationships, it is best to communicate with the understanding that you are each individuals with your own needs, strengths, and desires. Engage in verbal exchanges that are only worthy of your equal. To tap into each other's deepest desire, remember that men crave respect and appreciation, while women want to be loved and cherished. If you maintain this focus in your communication, your partner will most assuredly listen.

Whenever you catch yourself engaging in a parental manner with your partner, become aware and put the brakes on. Shift to a more productive way of being as fast as you can, such as attempting to understand your partner's situation, position, or perspective. Try to put yourself in your partner's shoes and see the situation from his or her unique vantage point. Never punish each other by purposefully withdrawing either attention or affection. If you need time apart, ask for it with a predetermined time of return. Avoid the urge to punish the other person. You are equal partners in your relationship, not parent and child.

Different Timing

Women often want to talk when their partner is relaxing in front of the television, watching a movie or a sporting event. This is *not* the best time to engage him in a conversation.

Men typically want their partner's attention at the end of a very long day or early in the morning when she is preoccupied with the children and the morning routine. This is not when she is best able to give him undivided attention.

Ideally, when your partner wants your undivided attention, you will recognize its importance and prioritize your other activities to accommodate him or her. If what you are doing at the time is more important, then perhaps you can let your partner know of your need to finish what you are doing and schedule a more convenient time to be completely available to him or her. When you do, treat this time as sacred. Protect it by not allowing anything to interfere.

When Angry: Shutting Down vs. Using Absolutes

Dr. Gray tells us that when women get upset, they tend to communicate in absolutes. They will say things such as, "You NEVER listen to me!" or "You ALWAYS side with your mother!" When men are upset, they tend to shut down and stop communicating.

Men, stop taking your woman literally when she is experiencing a heightened emotional state. She does not mean literally "always" or "never." She is merely expressing the level of frustration she is experiencing. Women, become more aware of this tendency and attempt to eliminate absolute language when communicating with your man.

As for your man shutting down, ladies, give him the time and space he needs to work it out. If you let him have what he needs, he will likely come back to you sooner. Men, you can also contribute to this solution if you let your woman know that you need some space but you will come back and discuss things once you have it worked out in your mind.

Optimism vs. Pessimism

A final area to examine is attributed more to personality differences rather than gender differences, and that is the degree to which you are either an optimist or a pessimist. If you find yourself paired with someone with the opposite outlook on life, you will most likely have some challenging communication.

The pessimist sees the negative in situations, while the optimist sees the positive. This can create conflict because the optimist will consider the pessimist to be unhappy and suspicious. The pessimist, on the other hand, will view the optimist as naïve and unrealistic.

A solution is to remember the richness in difference. While you each see the world differently, you can add a different perspective to your partner's perceptions. For pessimists, listening to your optimistic partner may help you see the hopeful side of a situation. For optimists, a pessimistic partner can easily point out potential pitfalls that you probably wouldn't consider.

As long as you stop judging your partner's perspective as wrong, you can open yourself to the possibility that he or she has perceptions that can help you see the situation more completely. You can complement rather than oppose each other. Instead of thinking that the situation is either optimistic or pessimistic, think of the situation as having elements of both perspectives that need to be examined. In this way, you can see your partner as a helpful person who can point out aspects you may not have thought of on your own.

How to Communicate

The best thing to do when you recognize some of these communication challenges in your relationship is to label them as what they are—differences—and stop assigning blame. You are two separate, unique individuals with your own style of communication. Understand that you have differences, seek information about these differences, and then learn to accept them. Stop trying to change your partner to be more like you. You'll probably be wasting your time, anyway. Instead appreciate your uniqueness and your partner's.

If you are in a committed relationship, it will be advantageous to understand your partner rather than labeling him or her as wrong. Embrace your differences because they are what make you uniquely you. Would you really want to go through life with someone exactly like you? How boring would that be?

So recognize your differences, seek to understand them, and then develop an appreciation for these differences. Make a concerted effort to support your partner by providing what he or she needs in the relationship. Look for the ways your differences enhance each of you individually and enrich your overall relationship.

In Dr. Covey's book, *7 Habits of Highly Effective People,* his 5th Habit is: "Seek first to understand, then to be understood." You need to understand your partner before asking him or her to understand you. Give the gift you want to receive. Try looking at the world through your partner's eyes. If you are the one reading this book, then I say *you* need to be the one to make the first move. Why? Because someone has to. If you wait for your partner, you may be waiting your entire life.

If you are reading this book, then I assume you are the one most interested in improving your relationship. That means *you* need to take control over the only thing you can control—YOU! Take the first step.

Find out what you can do to honor your partner's unique communication style. What can you do to improve communication between you? Now go do it!

Conflict in Communication

When you experience a disagreement, consider the possibility that your partner was not trying to deliberately wound you. Check to see if it's possible that your partner intended only good will but you misinterpreted the behavior as disrespectful.

Mitch and Lynn

I remember talking with a couple who had experienced a big misunderstanding and argument over one word, "Whatever." New into the relationship, Lynn was inviting Mitch to her house for dinner. However she did not want to give the impression that she was applying any undue pressure for him to come over. So she said, "I made some lasagna for dinner and there's plenty to eat if you aren't doing anything. Whatever." Mitch believes that when someone uses the word "whatever" it is intended as an insult or some type of disrespect. He became furious and Lynn had no idea what had gone wrong.

After Lynn apologized for saying something to upset Mitch, he was able to listen to her explanation of her use of the word "whatever." It was difficult for Mitch to understand because using "whatever" in her way was totally foreign to him. However, as he thought back to what he knew about Lynn and her overall respectful nature, he realized this was simply a misunderstanding. Finally they were able to enjoy a great dinner together.

These types of misunderstandings can occur. The idea is to remember who your partner shows himself or herself to be in most situations. Instead of jumping to conclusions that your partner means you harm or ill will, simply ask the question, "Did you mean that the way it sounded to me?"

When you talk to your loved one, take the time to consider how your words will sound to him or her. Ask yourself the question, *If I say what I am about to say, will it move me closer to or further away from this person*

I love? If the answer is further away, then find another way to communicate. If the answer is closer, then do it. If you don't know, ask.

Rules of Engagement

As a couple, you may want to establish some ground rules that you agree to follow whenever experiencing conflict in your relationship. Rules of Engagement will help you calmly discuss your disagreements and misunderstandings.

Use this, adapt it to suit your relationship, or start from scratch and write your own. However you do it, create Rules of Engagement for your relationship and honor them. Be certain if you have a rule that involves stopping something, you also spell out what you will do instead (see #5 below).

 Rules of Engagement Exercise

1. Take time alone to get clear about your grievance.
2. Formulate not only the problem, but clarify what you want your partner to do instead.
3. Agree on a time to discuss the issue without interruption. (Some couples in my research believe strongly that it is best not to go to bed with unresolved issues between you. If you concur, schedule a time before the end of day.)
4. Remember why you love this person and your motivation for working things out.
5. Never attack your partner. Do not criticize his or her character or sensitive subjects. Always treat each other with respect.
6. Listen with the intention of understanding your partner's position. You don't need to agree, but you at least want to understand his or her perspective.
7. Make the needs of your relationship a priority over your individual desires.

8. Ask your partner for what you want. If he or she agrees, then your problem is solved!
9. If your partner won't do as you wish, then be willing to adjust yourself in some way to accommodate your situation.
10. Seek to discover a solution you can both accept.

Vertical Conversations versus Dialogue

Dr. Harville Hendrix, father of Imago Therapy, says that couples need to stop having vertical conversations where one person "knows" what is right and is attempting to educate the other one. The balance of power is then clearly unequal, with the person who "knows" higher in the hierarchy than the one who doesn't. If couples want to accomplish effective communication, then they need to convert their vertical conversation to a dialogue.

In a dialogue, there is an even playing field. There is an optimal balance of power. Both partners are equal with equally valid points of view.

Dr. Hendrix also recommends that the topic of conversation change from being negative to a conversation filled with acknowledgement, acceptance, advocacy, affirmation, appreciation, and adoration. He says that conversations should never focus on either partner's limitations or faults.

Reducing the use of the Destructive Relationship Habits and increasing the use of the Healthy Relationship Habits discussed in chapter 4 will help transform vertical conversations into dialogue.

Chapter Eleven Summary

1. Men tend to process information internally; women tend to process externally.

2. Men are more intellectual, while women are more emotional.

3. Men value being respected while women want to be loved.

4. Men are direct communicators while women are more indirect with their communication.

5. Women turn their men into "partner improvement projects."

6. Men don't like to apologize.

7. Women hold grudges while men forget things the instant they are over.

8. When their partner is doing something they don't like, both men and women are capable of attempting to parent them into better behavior.

9. Men appear to have selective hearing, while women choose poor timing to have important conversations.

10. Women speak in terms of absolutes such as "always" and "never"; men take offense to this.

11. The first step to effective communication is to listen for understanding.

12. Develop appropriate Rules of Engagement to defer to during times of conflict.

13. Transform all vertical conversations into dialogue.

Proper Problem Identification

Whose Problem Is This, Anyway?

People are more comfortable with the emotion of anger
than the responsibility of acceptance.

—Marcus C. Gentry

It is not uncommon for couples to have difficulties in their relationship. Oftentimes people poorly define a problem in their lives. They either accept a problem as their own when it isn't, or they take a problem that is theirs and demand that their partner fix it.

Partners do things that drive each other crazy! In my work with couples, a common complaint of women is that their husbands don't put their dirty clothes in the hamper. They will leave their dirty clothes on the floor right next to the hamper but won't take that extra step to get them into the hamper. Even though this seems like such a simple issue, I have heard some women on the verge of divorce or a mental breakdown over it.

To be fair, I want to give men equal time here. One of the problems men complain about is their wife's inability to put gas in their car. She will often drive around with the red "low gas" light on and it drives husbands wild! This is another simple issue that can place a huge strain on many relationships.

When I ask the question, "Whose problem is it?" what I am really asking is, "Who is most upset by this problem?" Well, in the case of the dirty clothes, it's the woman who is upset. In the case of the empty gas tank, it's the man who is upset. Do you think the man is sitting at work upset because he left his dirty clothes on the floor? I doubt he even gives them a second thought once they are off his body. Nor do I think the woman is sitting at home thinking, "Oh darn, I forgot to stop for gas and now my sweetie is out driving our car and there's no gas!" No, she is likely to be equally oblivious to the gas situation.

Most of our suffering comes from having a problem with someone else. We create our own misery by attempting to force the other person into "fixing" the problem. Failure to take responsibility for the solution to our own problems results in misery and frustration. Proper problem identification is critical to the success of developing quality relationships. This occurs when the person who is most upset by the situation accepts ownership of the problem and the subsequent responsibility for its solution. Einstein said, "We can't solve problems by using the same kind of thinking we used when we created them." We need a new paradigm.

Once we can agree that the person with the problem is the person most upset by the issue, then we can get somewhere. However, what commonly happens is that if I am upset by something you do, then I am certain *YOU* are the problem and I am going to do everything within my power to ensure that you understand just how much of a problem you are. I am taking my problem and trying my hardest to make it your problem.

If you are on the receiving end of my frustration, you have four common responses:

1. You can recognize it's my problem but be willing to give me what I want

2. You can ignore my attempts at making you responsible for my issue

3. You can accept it's your problem and attempt to fix it

4. You can fight back and resist my attempts to make you the guilty party.

In the last three of these situations, we both lose. It may look like I win if you choose the third response, but do I really? Even if you fix the problem as I've identified it, how do you feel about me? Probably you are resentful of my methods. You may not like having to do something that you don't think is important. You may even find me unreasonable in my requests, thinking I don't have my priorities straight. This will do nothing to strengthen our relationship. So even if I think I've won something, our relationship has suffered. And so I lose.

The only two ways there can be a winning outcome is:

1. The person who is upset asks for a change and the other person agrees and implements the change because he or she understands and agrees with the request.

2. The person who is upset comes to accept that the problem belongs to him. Instead of trying to get his partner to fix his problem, he accepts responsibility for its solution.

Pick up the clothes. Fill the gas tank. Whatever the issue is, fix it. And while you're at it, leave the resentment behind. Don't get angry because your partner doesn't see the world the same way you do. Don't be frustrated that your priorities are different.

If you truly love your partner you will accept your loved one just as he or she is. Stop trying to change your partner. Fix the things that annoy you gratefully. Be happy that you have this wonderful person in your life!

When teaching a workshop on relationships, a woman came up to me afterwards to tell me that a good relationship is all about "accentuating the positive." When I asked her to explain further, she said that she used to get upset about the little things her husband didn't do around the house with regard to keeping things straightened up. She was complaining about him to another older woman, who asked her what positive qualities her husband possessed.

When the woman thought about it, she could list several. He didn't have affairs. He was a good provider. He was an excellent father. He took good care of her, taking her out often and on vacation once a year. He never drank or used drugs. He never raised his voice in anger toward her. Once the older woman heard the younger woman's list of positive attributes, she said, "Honey, you have a good man there. Are you sure you really want to be badgering him about picking up his clothes and running the vacuum? You have to learn to accentuate the positive." What great advice!

What would happen in your relationship if you accepted responsibility for the things you don't like and you accentuated the positive? You would be less frustrated and an easier partner to live with. Your relationship would prosper.

OK, It's My Problem, Now What?

Once you have properly identified the owner of the problem as being yourself, then the next question to ask yourself is, *If this is my problem, then who is responsible for the solution?* The answer is obvious. When you have a problem, naturally it's your job to fix it.

That is not to say that you don't have the right to ask for something you want from your partner. In fact, women are notorious for suffering in silence, expecting their partner to read their mind and give them what they desire. When men fail to tune in to their mental telepathy, women become angry thinking that their partner must not really love them. If you want to give your partner a chance to accommodate you, then you need to be very specific about what you want without blaming him.

Simply state what the problem is and how you would like it resolved. Ask for input from your significant other. Does your partner have any suggestions about what might work?

If you ask and nothing changes, then you will need to come up with your own solution for this problem. However, if you want to ask a second time, just for good measure, go ahead. But should you be tempted to ask a third time, be careful, you are bordering on nagging. Whatever you do, don't ask more than three times. Your partner has heard you and has not made your request a priority for whatever reason.

This means if you want to solve the problem, you are going to have to move into the process of self-evaluation. Ask yourself, *What do I want in this situation?* The answer will most likely be that you want your partner to do something different. If you want to apply the concepts of InsideOut

Empowerment, then you must instead turn your attention to what you can control—yourself.

Ask the follow up question, *If my partner were acting exactly the way I want, what would change for me?"* This answer will probably be something over which you have control. It might be that you would have a clean house, that you wouldn't have to nag, that you could stop worrying about your partner, or that you could drive the car without worrying about running out of gas. Do you see how these answers provide a problem you can solve on your own?

If you are like most people, you probably feel a strong resistance to this idea. This is because your sense of fairness tells you, *He or she should just do what I want. It's so simple. If he or she would simply do this, then everything would be fine.* The problem with this thinking is that you are taking one of your problems and putting the solution in the hands of someone who doesn't see it the same as you do. You can want your partner to comply, you can apply Destructive Habits, you can become miserable, but how will any of these behaviors solve the problem or help your relationship? Is anything you want your partner to do worth chipping away at your relationship? I think not or you wouldn't be reading this book.

The next questions to ask yourself are:

1. *If what I REALLY want is a better, healthy, supportive relationship with my partner and to solve my problem, what am I doing to move in that direction?*

2. *Is there anything I'm doing that is getting in the way of my goals?*

3. Once you have enumerated everything you are doing to both help and hinder your progress, ask yourself, *If I keep doing the things I've been doing, will I create the kind of relationship I want with my partner and solve my original problem?*

If the answer is no, then figure out how you can solve *your* problem using Healthy Relationship Habits with your partner. Solving the problem means you will either do or think something different to manage the situation.

Complete the form below using a current, past, or anticipated future situation where you are experiencing a problem with your partner.

 Self-Evaluation Exercise

Describe the problem: _____

_____

_____

Whose problem is it? _____

Have you asked for what you want? _____

How many times? _____

If your partner cooperated, what would change for you? _____

_____

_____

What are you doing to make that happen? _____

_____

_____

What are you doing that gets in the way? _____

_____

_____

If you keep doing what you've been doing, will you get what you want?

_____

_____

What else can you do to increase your chances of getting what you want?

_____

_____

Deal Breakers

Understanding that you own the problems that upset you doesn't change the fact that you have a problem. Usually there are practical things you can do to correct the problem and make your life, and the life of your partner, much happier.

Most couples get along well when times are good. But when things get tough they fight with each other, ignore each other, or leave each other. Leaving a relationship, especially one that is mostly satisfying, is a difficult decision. In fact, relationship expert Steve Toth says:

> When we leave a relationship we are passing on the opportunity for growth. We always think that the grass is greener on the other side. We just want a new partner—trade in the old one because we could not fix her or him.
>
> Running from a relationship when things get tough is what most of us want to do because we do not want to look at the core cause. "Walking through the fire"—staying is where the growth is. Experiencing what we have been resisting, going outside of our comfort zone is where the freedom is. Doing it alone without help is tough because we have blinders on and we can't see it. Most of us hire the worst coach there is: "ourselves," why? Because it's free, convenient and surely we will let ourselves off the hook.

You have a few options:

1. Continue the hard way of learning which is by following your life's journey-path, going from relationship to relationship until it gets so hard that everything in your life stops working to get your full attention. Now, you know that there is no escape from yourself. Now you see that the only thing that is common in all those relationships you have been in is: YOU! You have experienced so much pain and disappointment that now you are ready to look inside of you for the answers, which were there all along. But at what cost? What did you have to lose to get here?

2. Wait until some major life changing event occurs in your life such as: an accident, an illness, losing someone close to you,

someone dies. It seems from my experience that people become much more open and awake when a life-changing event happens and they stop looking for the answers outside of themselves and are ready to go within.

3. Save time, money and pain. Stop punishing yourself for something that happened a long time ago and transform the pain of your life now—get a coach to help you! Trust the process. If you could have done it on your own, you would have done it already.

While I mainly agree with what Toth says, especially the part about getting professional help, I surveyed my respondents about whether or not they had any deal breakers for their relationship: 31% said that there was nothing that would make them end their relationship. One person summed it up by saying, "As bad as some things could be, I think the worst would be ending this relationship."

The interesting thing about deal breakers is that people can self-righteously declare things to be deal breakers as long as they are not currently experiencing them. However, when confronted with a behavior they thought would end the relationship, suddenly things don't appear so black and white.

Thirty-nine percent of happy, satisfied couples said infidelity would be a deal breaker for them. An additional 11% thought cheating might be a deal breaker, but weren't sure. However, of the people who admitted one of them had had an affair, 100% thought infidelity would have been a deal breaker and it turns out it wasn't.

This can be explained by the simple fact that no one really knows how they will respond in a given situation until they are actually confronted with that situation. I don't believe that when one partner has an affair the relationship should necessarily come to an end. In fact, the next chapter discusses in great detail how a relationship can, in fact, survive an affair. There is much for both people to learn in that situation, as Toth explains.

Nineteen percent of respondents listed other deal breakers in the following order: physical abuse; child abuse; emotional abuse and pervasive lying (which were tied); drug and alcohol abuse; serious and/or violent crime; a major financial problem; a drastic change in belief system and partner wanting to end the relationship were tied; and loss of trust brought up the rear. While 33% of survey takers said that there was nothing that could end their relationship, many individuals have at least one non-negotiable that would cause them at least to think about ending their relationship.

I don't think it is best clinical practice for a professional to advocate for couples staying together when one of them has had a deal breaker violated. If someone in an abusive situation wants to leave, then he or she should leave. If another person experiences a severe financial violation and that was his or her deal breaker, then that person should be supported in whatever decision he or she wants to make regarding the relationship.

Sometimes a person reaches the point of making a behavior a deal breaker when the annoying behavior is displayed repeatedly. One incident alone wouldn't be a deal breaker. However when one partner continuously asks the other to stop doing something and the other person doesn't comply, the first person may want to end the relationship.

Tyler and Stephanie

Take the case of Tyler and Stephanie. Tyler had a habit of spending money on things Stephanie thought were unnecessary. Tyler preferred living in the moment without much regard to tomorrow, while Stephanie had a large concern about financial security for their future.

Repeatedly, she would ask him to stop. She even went as far as putting him on an allowance. But then he would work overtime, get paid under the table, and spend his extra money without even telling her he had any. He frequently played the lottery.

He would even borrow money from friends and family so he could invest in some small business that never seemed to work out. He would spend the money and end up with merchandise he couldn't sell.

One incident of frivolous spending would not have been a problem for Stephanie. Perhaps she could have tolerated many instances. But when she began to fear that they wouldn't have the money they needed for their mortgage payment, she filed for divorce.

If one partner cannot live with the repeated behavior of the other, then leaving may be the best option. Another example might be loss of respect. One partner is being disrespected on a regular basis. Perhaps in the beginning excuses were made for the disrespectful behavior, but over time the first person comes to realize that his or her partner is not going to change so they make the decision to end the relationship.

Dave and Marissa

Dave and Marissa seemed to often be in conflict. They fought about finances. They fought about the children. They fought about how to share the responsibility of household chores. They fought about their extended family members. It didn't seem that there was much upon which they agreed. Dave and Marissa had four young children. When they would argue, Dave often called Marissa names which she tolerated for ten years. Finally one day, she decided that she no longer wanted to be in a relationship where her husband continually disrespected her. She took the children and moved out. To this day they live separately but remain legally married, since neither believes in divorce. Living separately, they no longer argue and Marissa feels respected again.

It is important for individuals to know their bottom line of tolerance, even if that bottom line moves and changes. Know the minimum you require to stay in relationship with someone. If you are not at least receiving your minimum, you can take a serious inventory of the strength and health of your relationship and evaluate your choices: changing the relationship, accepting it the way it is, or leaving. Deal breakers don't always mean the relationship has to end. You can change your mind. But you should have an idea of what you need in a relationship to feel supported. When you are not receiving that support, you will need to reevaluate that relationship.

Chapter Twelve Summary

1. A large majority of relationship suffering comes from not owning the things that most upset us about our partners. When you are upset about something your significant other does or doesn't do, recognize that you are the one who owns the problem.

2. When you have a problem with your partner, you have the right and the responsibility to ask for what you want.

3. If your partner changes, great! Problem solved. But if he or she doesn't, then you need to become responsible for the solution instead of continuing to insist that your partner has to fix your problem.

4. Be clear about the non-negotiables (deal breakers) that you have in relationships.

5. If you encounter a deal breaker, determine what you are going to do about it based on what is best for you, your partner, and the relationship.

Trust

Can Your Relationship Survive an Affair?

> *If people could enjoy staying together as much*
> *as they fantasize about having sex with someone*
> *outside of their relationship then couples*
> *would keep from falling apart.*
>
> —Martin Dansky

One of the interesting findings of my research was that 87% of the respondents answered that they had never had an intimate relationship outside their primary committed relationship with their partners.

Further research would be needed to determine whether this was because loyalty and commitment are critical to successful relationships or whether the respondents did not trust me as a researcher; they might have been concerned that their answers would not be kept confidential. I would guess that most likely it was a combination of both.

Many people in happy and satisfied relationships consider trust, loyalty, commitment, and monogamy to be high on their list of requirements. However it should be noted that only 39% of respondents said that infidelity would be a deal breaker in their relationship; 31% did not list it as an absolute deal breaker.

Furthermore, most of the people who knew that their partner had had an affair were able to work through their issues successfully and stay in their relationship—despite the fact that initially they had believed infidelity would end their relationship.

In my work, I am often asked whether it's possible to make a relationship work after an affair and if so, how is that accomplished? Every relationship expert I interviewed agreed that relationships can definitely survive and even get stronger after an affair. This chapter explores infidelity and provides different perspectives and some formulas for successfully moving beyond an affair in your relationship.

How Does One Define an Affair?

An affair is often defined as engaging in sexual activity with a person outside your committed relationship. As the world saw with President Clinton, this idea was challenged when he claimed not to have had sex with Monica Lewinsky when, in fact, they had oral sex. Is having oral sex considered an affair? How about intense kissing or petting? Do internet relationships count? What about pornography? How about an intensely intimate platonic relationship with potential sexual interest?

These are all great questions that should be discussed with your partner before making a commitment. What matters is what you, as an individual, define as a betrayal of your trust.

What the Experts Say

Two relationship experts have very interesting points to make about affairs.

Dr. Kan states that a quality relationship exists when both partners unconditionally support the personal growth of each other. If you love your partner unconditionally and totally support his growth and development, and your partner believes that he needs to have an intimate relationship with another person to accomplish that, then you will support that arrangement. Obviously, few couples truly reach this level of unconditional love.

Dr. Hendrix says that in all his work with couples, he has never encountered a couple where only one partner was having an affair. He says that if you look below the surface you will find that the "victims" were having "affairs" of their own, but their "affairs" were more socially acceptable. Partners can have "affairs" with their children, their work, their extended family, their friends, their pets, and other things. Any area of your life that takes precedence over your intimate, committed relationship can be considered an affair. However in most cultures, an intimate, sexual affair with another person is considered far more despicable than devoting too much time to one's children or work. Society approves more of these distractions, thus vilifying the partner who has an intimate affair with another person.

Dr. Hendrix says, "Infidelity is a co-creation designed to regulate intimacy by acting out their anxiety in ways that involved them with other people. . . . There are always two affairs. They are always co-created."

If your partner had an affair and you consider yourself the "victim," you may want to do some soul searching to determine if there was anything you were prioritizing over your relationship. This is not to place blame on you. It is merely to distribute the responsibility more evenly for what happened and equalize the efforts for repairing the damage.

If you want your relationship to survive this affair and even grow stronger, then sharing the responsibility for what happened in your relationship is a healthy first step, as outlined in the section later in this chapter called, "Working through the Trauma."

Cultural Differences

Throughout history until present day, many cultures and religions have recognized and condone the practice of plural marriages. Certain couples have agreed to have an "open marriage," where additional partners are acceptable within the context of their relationship. Other couples will invite outside sexual partners to share their bed with them at certain times.

The point is: monogamy is a culturally generated idea. If you were raised in a culture or religion that promotes monogamy, then you will likely believe it is the right way to be in a committed relationship. Consequently, your beliefs and your perception of right and wrong will determine how you experience and even define an affair within your relationship.

If you don't have the cultural or religious belief that monogamy is critical to the success of your relationship or to your own self-esteem, then you will likely not be traumatized to discover that your partner is engaged in an affair. Nor will you experience guilt if you engage in an affair.

I include this section because cultural and religious beliefs can be challenged. People are capable of changing their value system when they question the validity of their current belief system. They can go from believing infidelity is wrong to accepting affairs as part of their relationship, if that is their desire.

That said, most people I work with are from a culture that supports monogamy. As a result, when they learn of their partner's affair they tend to experience great trauma to their psyche. The betrayal is strong; trust is compromised; and the partners are not sure if they will ever be able to rebuild their relationship.

Can a couple rebuild their relationship after an affair? The answer is yes, when certain conditions are met.

So you've just learned that your partner was having an affair. Whether you suspected all along and just received confirmation, or you were suddenly confronted with irrefutable evidence, you most likely feel hurt, disappointed, angry, and devastated. These emotions are flooding your brain with chemicals, making it difficult for you to think clearly.

Steps for Recovery Exercise

1. Calm down so you can think clearly. Take deep breaths. Walk away momentarily. Spend some time apart.

   Research shows that when you are in a highly emotional state, you are unable to engage in higher order thinking. Your brain goes into reactive mode where you either fight, flee, or freeze. You need to let go of these emotions so you can make wise decisions.

2. Get Clear about Your Options.

There are three options when experiencing problems with your relationship: you can change it, accept it, or leave it.

a. If you want to *change* your relationship, there are two ways to go about this. You can attempt to manipulate your partner into doing what you want. Once you have asked and he has not complied, you typically resort to Destructive Relationship Habits. Or, you can attempt to change the situation by changing yourself: doing something different, changing your perception, or changing your expectations.

b. If you decide to *accept* the relationship as it is, you need to recognize what happened, realize that your partner is not perfect, and decide to move on. This option means that you have given up the idea that you are going to change your partner. Again, two options exist: you accept the affair as a mistake and together decide to rebuild your relationship. Or you recognize that your partner may always be unfaithful and accept his infidelity because you have enough other benefits from your relationship.

c. If you decide to *leave*, you can leave emotionally or physically. Emotional leaving involves staying together on a day-to-day basis but having little to no emotional investment in the relationship. You have built a wall to protect yourself and you won't let your partner in. The other option is to leave the relationship physically. This means you end the relationship and each go your own separate ways.

3. Once you decide which direction you want to go, know that it does not have to be a permanent decision. You may first choose to try to change your partner's behavior and your own, and then later decide to leave the relationship. Or you may decide to leave the relationship emotionally, and later change your own perceptions

and behavior so that you become emotionally involved again. There are any number of possibilities.

4. Once you've made your decision, stay true to your desires. Don't allow other people to sway your thinking. Remember, they are not you. They have not lived your life. They don't necessarily have the same value system you have. They can only know what's best for them, not what's best for you. Only you can truly know. So once you become clear, stay true to your inner knowing.

5. It is always helpful to get the unbiased support you need to consciously implement your chosen option. There may be many people who are willing to support you in their way but their way may be biased. Find someone who will support you in following through on what you want—who doesn't already have preconceived ideas about what might be best for you. A good life coach or counselor can help you move through these steps.

Remember, if you find yourself feeling betrayed by your life partner, you are not at the mercy of his or her actions, or your emotions. You can make conscious, intentional decisions to move yourself in the direction you most want to go.

The next section outlines three options that couples have for managing affairs. Certainly not every option will fit your relationship, but they are listed here because they have worked for others.

The Benefits Outweigh the Difficulties

Couples have been able to move past an affair, or even multiple affairs, when the benefits from their relationship outweigh the difficulty they experience from accepting the affairs. Whether or not you believe that you could do this, it has worked for many couples.

There are people who know that their partner engages in outside affairs and yet they stay in the relationship for a variety of reasons. One reason might be financial. It would be difficult and costly to dissolve the marriage so they opt to stay. Or they may like the financial benefits of the relationship and overlook the affairs. Others may stay because they don't want to split up the family and deal with visitation rights with their children. Others may overlook affairs because they are not interested in sexual activity and are happy that their partner has alternative ways to satisfy that need. Others enjoy the benefit and attention they receive from being the victim or injured party.

There may be any number of reasons to stay in a relationship where infidelity is occurring. Both partners might still be happy and satisfied with their relationship because they are getting what they want and need from it.

From the outside looking in, you may say to a friend, "You deserve better than that! Don't you have any self-respect? How can you put up with that?" When a person comes to me for coaching because their partner is having an affair, or multiple affairs, I generally ask the following questions.

1. Do you expect your partner to change?

2. How long have you been waiting for him or her to stop having affairs?

3. Is it likely that waiting longer will change his or her behavior?

4. Are you willing to accept your partner's infidelity in exchange for the other benefits that you receive from the situation?

5. Can you live with this and still be happy and satisfied in your relationship?

When people answer yes to the last question, I am able to help them get to a place where the infidelity does not overshadow the entire relationship. However, if they want their partner to change and can't feel good unless that happens, then they generally need to get out of the relationship.

You may wonder how people who are happy and satisfied in their relationship can have an outside affair. This can be explained by the fact that no one person can be everything to another, meeting all of their needs.

Perhaps the relationship works perfectly. The partners are happy with each other, have multiple common interests, and appreciate the other's hard work and parenting styles. They are getting everything they want from their relationship and are completely happy and satisfied. And having an affair helps them stay happy and attracted in their committed relationship.

You can learn to accept infidelity in your relationship if the trade off is worth it. You can learn to think about it differently and not feel so personally injured. It may not be easy to do, but if the relationship is important enough to you, you can get to a place of peace with it.

Maintaining Secrecy

Another way to successfully manage an affair is to keep it a secret. Many people will reject this alternative because they value truth as paramount in a relationship. (Remember, 49% of the couples surveyed said trust was the number one thing they expected in their relationship.) I am not talking about maintaining a long term affair and keeping it secret. I'm talking about people who recognized that their affair was damaging their relationship, ended it, and decide to forever keep the secret from their partner.

I have known people who have had affairs and who have successfully managed their relationship by recognizing their mistake, ending their affair, and maintaining the secret so that their partner never learns of the affair. When I interview these couples, both partners say that they are happy and satisfied in their relationship.

This may not match your value system. You may believe that the injured party has a right to know or may find out at some later date. However, if the secret stays secret, then the relationship can survive quite well. Of course, the person keeping the secret must be prepared in the case the affair becomes known.

When the person who engaged in the affair opts to keep it secret, it isn't always for selfish reasons. Many of the couples I have worked with who chose this path did it out of concern for their partner. They didn't want to hurt their partner. They recognized that they made a mistake and are committed to never engaging in another affair. Since that part of their life is over, it seems that it would only serve to hurt the other person to confess. So they opt to carry the secret to spare their partner pain.

Working through the Trauma

Many who ask me the question, "How can a relationship survive an affair?" are really asking, "How can I regain the trust I once had?" This question is multi-faceted. Let's start by outlining the three-step process for moving beyond an affair:

The first step is for both people to realize that their relationship is important enough for them to attempt to heal from the trauma. Consequently, both partners recognize the role they each played in the breakdown of their relationship.

The second step is for both partners to genuinely want to correct their actions that contributed to this breakdown. For the person who had the affair, this means ending the illicit relationship. For the other partner, it means making the committed relationship a priority over whatever else was taking precedence.

The third step is forgiveness. This happens when both parties recognize that neither of them is perfect and that they are both capable of making hurtful mistakes. The affair does not have to become the one event of monumental importance in their relationship. The person who had the affair needs to become more forthcoming with information about his or her activities. The person who was the victim needs to stop punishing his or her partner through guilt and blame and instead begin to trust again.

Step One: Do You Want to Save Your Relationship?

Of the couples I surveyed, 49% listed trust as a critical component of their relationship. It's amazing to me how this theme of trust keeps presenting itself in my work.

I was talking to one of my clients, Susan, about her readiness to begin a new relationship. Susan had been divorced for about five years and believed that she was ready to start dating but nothing was happening for her.

I asked her if there was something holding her back. She is an attractive and fun-loving individual. I suggested that maybe she was allowing her ex-husband to hold too much power over her emotions for her to engage in a relationship with someone new.

She thought about that and realized that when her husband had an affair with a much younger woman, it totally shook the foundation of her self-esteem. If she doesn't like herself, then how could someone else be attracted to her?

So often, when your trust is shattered, you tend to ask yourself: *What's wrong with me? Why did someone I love betray me? Why didn't I see it coming?*

Instead of thinking that there is something innately wrong with you, your energy is best spent examining what part you might have had in the breakdown of the relationship and taking responsibility for your part. Both of you allowed something else to assume greater importance than your relationship.

Some people make mistakes, learn from them, and never repeat them. While it is possible to regain trust, it is a challenge and may require some time. Many people don't have the patience and commitment to work through their issues, but it certainly is possible.

When it comes to relationships, so many people play it safe. They have been hurt before. They don't trust easily. They fear the game. It is very similar to an injured athlete. Whenever a professional athlete returns from an injury, he has a choice to make. He either plays full out as he did before his injury or he cautiously protects the body part that was hurt.

The athletes who play full out have the potential to get right back to their pre-injury glory. However, they also run the risk of re-injury that could potentially end their career. The athletes who protect themselves will never again attain that pinnacle of success they had experienced prior to the injury. However, they create the potential of going the distance, safely.

There are definite advantages to each approach. It really is more of an individual style. In which method do you engage? Do you play all out, risking it all? Or are you playing it safe?

Trust is actually a verb. It's not something your partner earns or loses. It's a decision you make that can be seen in your thoughts and behavior. It really comes down to which is most important to you: trust or self-protection?

If you are more concerned with keeping yourself safe, you probably won't trust because you are afraid of being hurt. However, can you really protect yourself from pain? Won't you still be hurt to learn of a loved one's deception? Without trust, you will never achieve the level of intimacy a trusting relationship provides. What will you really lose by trusting?

The most important thing not to lose is your self-respect. You are a worthy person. Spend some time engaging in some self-nurturing behavior. Learn to love yourself again. Do not allow your self-respect to be based on the whims and fantasies of another person.

If you have learned of your partner's affair and he or she isn't likely to stop this behavior, do you want to stay in relationship with your partner even if he or she doesn't change? If not, then you need to seriously consider ending your relationship. There is no point torturing yourself. However, if you are willing to stay because there are so many other benefits and you can change your perception of your partner's infidelity so that it doesn't hurt you, then you can make this work.

If your partner is genuinely interested in working things out with you and has ended his or her affair with a promise to never do it again, are you willing to do whatever it takes to work through this? If not and you are going to continue to punish your partner, while feeling angry, hurt and bitter, then you may want to consider ending the relationship. This punishing dynamic will only cause you both pain and will likely drive your partner further away from you.

However, if you are truly interested in repairing the damage done, and if saving your relationship is your priority, then you have taken the first step. Whenever you experience doubt, fear, or anger along the way, remind yourself of your highest goal: repairing your relationship.

Step Two: Correct the Behavior

When you have accepted responsibility for your part in the affair, whether you were the "perpetrator" or the "victim," the next step is about corrective action. If you are committed to your relationship, you will do your part to correct whatever behavior you engaged in that created the problem. In other words, you will consciously and consistently make your commitment to your significant other a priority, regardless of what your partner does.

This is not time for a tit for tat situation. You don't want to hold back action, waiting to see what your partner contributes; this would likely result in a stalemate. Once you have determined in Step One that you really want to get your relationship back on track, you don't want to let anything get in the way of your ferocious determination to change whatever patterns of behavior lead to this situation.

If you were the one involved in the affair, end it with no thoughts of maintaining contact with the other person. If your partner is having difficulty trusting you, then be open about everything with him or her in an attempt to allay the fear. Allow your life to become an open book. Aim for transparency in the relationship.

If you were the partner engaged in a socially acceptable affair, then you must reprioritize your life so that your partner and your relationship become of paramount importance. Cut back on the time you spend working. Get some assistance with your children if they are monopolizing your time. Reduce the time you spend on other things and recommit to your primary relationship with your partner.

Step Three: Forgiveness

If you have fully committed to the repair of your relationship, then you must forgive each other for the problems you both created. How do you forgive? You realize that what happened was a mistake and not meant to hurt you intentionally. You begin to trust again. It will become easier to trust again once you have both performed the committed actions from Step 2.

People have been taught to believe that trust is a commodity to be earned by others. Once your partner has passed certain tests, you feel safe to extend your trust. I would like you to entertain the idea that trust can be used as a verb, rather than a noun.

When you are involved in a relationship and you say that you trust that person, you are using "trust" as a verb. Then trust is not just a thing you extend to a person like a gift; it is followed up with behaviors.

When you trust your partner, you have faith that he or she intends to do the right thing. You believe that your partner is faithful and loyal. You don't need constant reassurance of this—you just know. If doubts creep in, you can quickly and easily put them to rest by asking yourself what you believe to be true about your partner.

What you don't do is constantly grill your partner about where and with whom he or she has been. You don't have your partner followed looking for proof of infidelity. You don't snoop around in his or her personal belongings or private places. You trust that your partner can be trusted.

Whether you trust has so much more to do with who you are as a person than it does with who your partner is. When you are secure in yourself and know that you are worthy to receive love, it is natural to trust, even if that trust has been violated.

Deciding to trust again means you must stop punishing your partner. We punish in several ways. Often we punish with our emotions: We are angry, hurt, jealous, and insecure. These emotions are all designed to send a clear message of guilt to our partner. "Look what you did to me." This is the worst form of punishment. Create the self-talk necessary to get through the rough spots.

If you want more trust in your life, you have to be more trusting and more worthy of trust. You can't get from others what you don't possess yourself. Ask yourself: *Am I a trustworthy person? Does my partner realize that I have integrity and can be trusted? Do I extend trust to him or her?* Change begins with you. Remember the quote from Mahatma Gandhi, "You must be the change you want to see in the world."

Trust your partner. Trust yourself. And finally, trust in the universal order of things—in a divine spirit, if you will. If you have total and complete trust in the Universal Spirit or your Higher Power then that trust can never be betrayed. The Universal Spirit will always provide you with what you need.

Of course, it's always possible that you will recommit yourself to your partner and he or she will violate your trust again. It can happen. If it does, don't allow that to shake your self-confidence. You are right to trust the person with whom you are involved. If your partner doesn't deserve your trust, in time this will be revealed to you and then you can forgive— whether or not you choose to stay with the person. But if your choice is to forgive and stay, then make "trust" into an action verb once more.

As a powerful testimony to the power of forgiveness, I include a quote from one of the survey respondents, Amelia. She said, "Yes, [I had one affair], very brief . . . I told him. He said it didn't matter and he would always trust me and never bring it up again. He never has (it's been 25 years since and not once.) He is a man of his word!" In fact, Amelia's husband didn't even mention her having an affair in his survey responses. It's as if he wiped it right from his memory. What a gift to give his partner—the gift of total forgiveness.

Let go of the wrong that was done. Trust in yourself again. And ultimately trust in the Universal Spirit to always and forever provide you what you need when you need it. You will discover a sense of peace and calm that will sustain you through the challenging times.

Chapter Thirteen Summary

1. Affairs are defined differently by different people. Find out how you and your partner define it.

2. There are cultural and religious factors that will determine how you define infidelity.

3. When you learn of an affair that's impacting your relationship, make your decisions with a clear, calm mind.

4. If you and your partner are interested in preserving your relationship, then follow the three-step process to survive and thrive after an affair:

   a. Decide what you want.

   b. Take action to correct the behavior.

   c. Forgive your partner.

Differences

Conflict, Tolerance, Acceptance, Appreciation

> Our greatest strength as a human race is our
> ability to acknowledge our differences;
> our greatest weakness is our failure to embrace them.
>
> —Judith Henderson

Dr. Hendrix says, "People fall in love with people who are incompatible. Then, their differences amplify that incompatibility. They need to engage in conversation about those differences to determine how to stay in relationship with each other, while learning [their own] individual lessons."

Unless you commit to a person who is the mirror image of you (which, if possible, would probably be incredibly boring), you will experience differences in your relationship. One of you may like spicy food, the other bland. One may think that toilet paper should be pulled over the top of the holder, the other from beneath. One may squeeze the toothpaste from the middle of the tube, the other from the end. You may have differing ideas about ideal temperature. One may prefer no clutter; the other may create piles of clutter everywhere. One may want a cat and the other may be allergic. And these are just some small differences. Imagine the bigger ones. You may have different pictures of vacation destinations. You may disagree on parenting practices. Finances may be a strain—one is a spender, the other a saver. You may not like each other's friends or families. The list can go on and on.

This chapter is devoted to looking at the four positions you can take in response to differences between you and your partner:

1. Conflict
2. Tolerance
3. Acceptance
4. Appreciation

Differences often create conflict. Once recognized, couples can make a decision to tolerate those differences. An even higher form of managing difference comes from acceptance. And finally, appreciation of difference can be a pinnacle to which you aspire.

Conflict

One of the biggest impediments to appreciating differences comes from our inherent propensity to be self-righteous. In other words, when there are differences, people tend to dig their heels in and polarize, believing that they are absolutely, unequivocally correct.

Dr. Hendrix says that couples can use any difference as an excuse to act out their fears or to regulate the intimacy between them. He says, "Difference is the number one casualty of a relationship. Most couples have difficulty allowing difference without judgment. . . Difference is difference and that's ok."

Differences can be as simple as how to thread the roll of toilet paper on the holder, or they can be much more significant. There are cultural, religious, political, and age differences. You may have different beliefs about how to raise the children, how to pay bills, how to save money, and how to be intimate, to name a few.

There appears to be a rigidity that is built into our psyche. From the time we are born, we begin an acculturation process. We are taught by those close to us how the world works—what's right and what's wrong. If we could remove ourselves from this acculturation process, we would

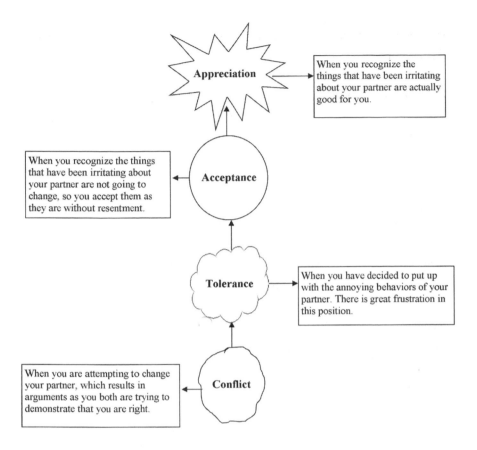

When you recognize the things that have been irritating about your partner are actually good for you.

When you recognize the things that have been irritating about your partner are not going to change, so you accept them as they are without resentment.

When you have decided to put up with the annoying behaviors of your partner. There is great frustration in this position.

When you are attempting to change your partner, which results in arguments as you both are trying to demonstrate that you are right.

quickly learn that there are many models of how the world works and many shades of gray on what constitutes right and wrong. Having this perspective would make it much more difficult for us to be righteous.

Whenever you begin to see your partner's attitudes, beliefs, and behaviors as dead wrong, you need to stop and ask yourself the question, *Is he really wrong or is this just a difference of opinion?* When you realize that it almost always is just a difference of opinion, then you can approach the situation with curiosity as opposed to righteous judgment. Instead of judging your partner to be wrong, you begin to wonder about his perspective. You try to understand his position, rather than convincing him to see things your way.

Whenever you take a righteous position, you will inevitably have conflict in your relationship.

Tolerance

If you can get past your righteousness, you can move up to the next position: tolerance. When you are tolerant, you aren't happy about your partner's differences but you are willing to put up with them. You may have explored his or her position with curiosity and not found any validity there. You still think your partner is wrong. However, you are willing to tolerate the situation, perhaps because you think that your partner's positive qualities are worth the trade off. However, you maintain a degree of frustration and a strong desire for your partner to change.

Whenever you are tolerating something in another, you can't help using Destructive Relationship Habits around this issue. You may argue that you aren't using Destructive Relationship Habits because you no longer say anything about the subject. However, I'd wager that your nonverbal behavior is sending out some not so subtle signs of disapproval: the silent treatment, eye rolling, deep sighs, loud exaggerated movements, facial grimaces, etc. These nonverbal behaviors are communicating volumes to your partner about your disapproval.

One possible explanation for why it is so difficult for couples to allow differences in their relationship is that they think if they allow their partner's reality to exist, then their reality will be diminished in some way. While this is not true, the fear of losing one's identity can be very strong.

Tolerance can be very frustrating. For the benefit of your peace of mind and your relationship, you may want to move up to the next position of acceptance.

Acceptance

For a good definition of acceptance, I like to quote Reinhold Niebuhr's Serenity Prayer: "God grant me the serenity to accept the things I cannot change, courage to change the things I can and the wisdom to know the difference."

Let's start with wisdom, the part of this prayer pertaining to the understanding of the things you can control. Whose behavior can you control? If you are like most people, you don't like answering this question because you know you can't control your partner's behavior, no matter how much you would like to. However, you do know the only person's behavior you can control is your own. This is wisdom.

The next part is courage to change what you can. When you understand that the only person's behavior you can control is your own, then you can stop thinking about changing your partner. Do you have enough courage to change your negative, perhaps controlling, responses to your partner's differences? If the answer is yes, then you may be ready to move into the acceptance position.

What does acceptance look like? It looks and feels like serenity, just as Niebuhr stated. In order to accept, you must let go of all anger, frustration, and resentment that your partner thinks, believes, or behaves differently from you. You must see the whole person and embrace him or her as an individual with strengths, differences, and faults, and love that person fully and completely, not conditionally. You will know you've achieved acceptance when you feel peaceful. Acceptance is a gift that you give to your partner which offers huge benefits for you as well.

If you are at acceptance but would like to take your relationship to the next level, then you can advance to appreciating differences.

Appreciation

When you begin appreciating your partners' differences you have not only accepted them but are now looking for the lesson or gift that they offer. If your partner is a spender, perhaps the lesson for you is to be more spontaneous and carefree sometimes. If your partner is a saver, your lesson might be to spend some time thinking of and planning for the future.

If your partner makes some messes in the house that you don't appreciate, then perhaps your lesson is to appreciate his or her presence in your life and take care of the mess yourself, or just stop fretting over it.

Suppose you and your partner are at different ends of the parenting continuum. One of you is permissive and the other is dictatorial. It is easy to polarize around the parenting issues and begin to believe that your partner is the one who is causing all your children's problems. Of course, this is not true. You need to find something to appreciate about your partner's parenting style. If you are the dictatorial parent, your partner may be more relaxed in the parenting role and may have a better relationship with your children. If you are the permissive one, then your partner brings safety and boundaries to the parent/child role.

Malcolm and Kate

Let's revisit the story of Malcolm and Kate who were involved in a committed interracial relationship. Kate is an entrepreneur and Malcolm is an actor/entertainer. Malcolm often traveled in pro-Black circles where a white female was not easily accepted. In an attempt to save both of them unnecessary stress, Malcolm would often go places without Kate.

Initially, Kate tolerated this but she took every opportunity to let him know that this behavior hurt her. Over time, she came to better understand his position. While she didn't agree with him, she understood how he saw things and she came to accept his position.

When I challenged her to move from acceptance to appreciation, she realized that if he took her with him into situations where he was most uncomfortable, he may come to value their relationship less. She also realized that if she were invited to all his social and business activities, she would have no time to develop her own business and realize her mission for her own life. She was able to find how his behavior was benefiting her and move into the position of appreciation. Additionally, developing a greater understand of pro-Black culture helped her professionally as she facilitates diversity workshops.

The Hendrickses says that we all come from a different culture. People need to see their partner as an ally. They need to see every interaction with their partner as an opportunity to learn rather than something that needs to be changed, controlled, or fixed in the other person. This creates an opportunity to enhance their life experiences rather than to focus on getting their partner to be like them. People must be willing to learn what natural gifts their partners bring.

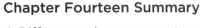

Chapter Fourteen Summary

1. Differences between partners can create serious conflict in the relationship.

2. When couples tire of arguing, they will often move to the tolerance position of managing differences, where they are "putting up" with the irritations of each other.

3. Moving from tolerance to acceptance brings great peace. Understanding you can't make someone else change and loving them anyway is a gift to your relationship.

4. Some couples get to an enlightened place of recognition that in their differences is an opportunity for great growth and come to appreciate those differences.

Negotiating for the Win/Win/Win

Everyone's a Winner

Conflict plus love equals growth.

—Westy Egmont

There will be times when you and your partner will have different ideas of what you want. In these cases, you have several options:

1. You can continue to be at odds, trying to convince your partner to do things your way.

2. You can give in to your partner's wishes without regard to what you want, often leading to resentment.

3. You can work together as a team to negotiate so you can both get what you need, and your relationship will be strengthened—hence the win/win/win.

Dr. Hendrix says, "Conflict is growth trying to happen." The path you choose will determine whether or not positive growth will occur.

The Native American Talking Stick

"The talking stick has been used for centuries by many American Indian tribes as a means of just and impartial hearing. The talking stick was commonly used in council circles to designate who had the right to speak . . . Whoever holds the talking stick has within his hands the sacred power of words. Only he can speak while he holds the stick; the other council members must remain silent." (www.acaciart.com/stories/archive6.html)

This is a very valuable concept in relationships as well. The talking stick represents the Healthy Relationship Habit of listening. It isn't just about hearing what a person says—it's actually about listening for understanding. The way Stephen Covey recommends using the talking stick in his book, *The 8th Habit*, is that the person with the talking stick holds it until he is satisfied that the other people in the room at least understand his point of view. There doesn't have to be agreement, just understanding.

Once the person with the talking stick feels sufficiently understood, then he relinquishes it to someone else to speak his or her piece. This works especially well when couples are having difficulty and both partners think they are right. If they wish to use the talking stick, they can flip a coin to determine who goes first. Let's say the woman wins the toss. She takes the talking stick and explains her point of view. She gives the stick to her partner only when he demonstrates that he understands her point of view. Then he gets to explain his perspective.

In many relationships, the need for power gets in the way of effective communication. When you have a conflict in your relationship, your natural inclination is to convince your partner to see things your way. At the same time your partner is trying to convince you that his or her way is right. Is it any wonder people who approach problem solving in this way face some very real challenges?

Entering any negotiation with the mindset that you are right and the other person is wrong is a recipe for disaster. This mindset creates a lose/lose situation. You may succeed in getting your partner to do things your way but in doing so you damage your relationship through coercion. If your partner is successful at getting you to do things his or her way, then you will likely feel misunderstood, resentful, and bullied.

It is crucial to intimate relationships to enter a negotiation with the idea that you want to gather all the information in order to understand all positions and thus make the best decision possible.

Whenever you and your partner have an issue to work out, you are already an expert on your position. You are quite clear about what you want. There is no wavering in that regard. However, somehow—you may have difficulty fathoming how—your partner wants something different. This is the perfect time to use the concept of the talking stick. Some couples find it helpful to actually have an object that gets passed between them representing the talking stick. Others do not need an object to hold but can engage in the spirit of the talking stick by just taking turns explaining one's position.

Use a method of chance to determine who will speak first. The person who wins gets the literal or figurative talking stick. This means that person gets to explain his or her position until satisfied that the partner understands it. It's important to remember that understanding does not necessarily mean agreement.

The best way to demonstrate understanding is to repeat back in your own words what your partner is saying to you. If you satisfy your partner's need for understanding, then your partner will pass the stick to you and allow you to have your say. If your partner is not feeling heard, then he or she will keep the stick and continue to talk until you can successfully explain your understanding of your partner's thoughts and feelings back to him or her.

Once you pass the stick you must be quiet. Your task during this time is simply to try to understand how your partner sees the situation. Work hard to gain this understanding by adopting an attitude of curiosity instead of judgment. When you think you understand where your partner is coming from, communicate that understanding in your own words.

If your partner recognizes that you do, in fact, understand sufficiently, then you will be ready to move to the next step of finding a solution you can both accept.

Bill and Carolyn

Bill and Carolyn are a happily married couple who always vacationed at the beach each summer with their family. Every year, Bill noticed that Carolyn got quite testy right before going on vacation—and it seemed to be more than the typical pre-vacation stress. After several years of noticing this pattern, he decided to ask her about it.

Carolyn was actually quite angry. She had been going on the annual trek to the beach just because that was what Bill wanted to do. He had never asked her what her idea of the perfect vacation was. He and his family had always vacationed at the beach and he couldn't fathom any other type of vacation.

He really wanted to work this out with Carolyn because normally she was very pleasant and he didn't like the idea that their vacation made her unhappy. He decided to listen.

As it turned out, Carolyn didn't really mind going to the beach. She loved the ocean and being on the beach with their children. However, the problem was that back then most beach house rentals weren't air conditioned. Carolyn has a terrible time with the heat. If Bill could figure out a way to keep her cool, she would love going to the beach.

That year, Bill decided to strap an air conditioner on their car when they left for the beach. He put it in their bedroom window at the beach house and they have been vacationing happily ever since. Of course today most beach houses come equipped with air conditioning so Bill doesn't have to travel with his own unit anymore.

This is an example of how two people were able to work things out by simply listening to each other.

Getting to a Solution You Can Both Accept

In *The 8th Habit*, Stephen Covey discusses finding "The Third Alternative," which occurs when two people come to the negotiation table with the mindset that not only is it possible to find a way for both of them to win, it is unacceptable to proceed any other way. Covey says, "It's win/win or no deal." He won't participate in negotiations where both people don't get what they want or at least what they need.

The human need for power creates self-righteousness. Once you take that position, you are unable to see anything but your own view. The power need further pushes you to *have* to get what you want. If you lose the argument or have to settle for something less, then you believe you are weak, powerless, and unable to stand up for yourself. This perception gets in the way of searching for an acceptable alternative to what you want.

You know what *you* want. You also know that what your partner wants is standing in the way of getting what you want. When this happens, the exchange with your partner becomes about winning. There is no room for you to take your partner's needs into consideration or attempt to find a win/win/win solution. This is not the time to decide you have to win at any cost. Your cost just might be your relationship, or at the very least, harmony in your relationship.

Once you have engaged the technique of the talking stick, then you are ready to work out the issue of how you can both get what you want. This is not a case of compromising. If you or your partner feels as if you are compromising, then the negotiation is considered lose/lose. You are each giving up something you want. The idea is to find a genuine solution where you can both have what you need. It may not look like the solution you wanted when you began the negotiation but when you reach consensus, both you and your partner should be happy and satisfied with what you have agreed upon. And your relationship will be strengthened by going through this process.

There are very rarely any true dilemmas, where one of you getting what you want inevitably means that the other can't have what he or she wants. If you believe you have a true dilemma, then get some professional help from a spiritual advisor, a therapist, or a coach. Since they are objective, they may be able to see something that you can't because you are in the midst of it.

When you've used the idea of the talking stick to truly understand the situation from each other's point of view, you can easily formulate solutions that may appeal to your partner and still provide you with what you need.

The idea is to brainstorm all options. You never know when the seed for the solution will appear in a thought that seems outrageous. When you first start, do not censor the free-flow of suggestions and possibilities. Simply operate in the spirit of finding an equitable way for you to both get what you want.

Solutions: Eric and Kelly are partners who each get only one week of vacation a year. He wants to go to the mountains and she wants to go to the beach. It can appear to be an insolvable problem until you really focus on finding the win/win/win solution. Anytime a couple figures out how to find a solution that satisfies both partners, not only do they both win but their relationship becomes stronger.

There are several solutions to this seeming vacation dilemma. They can find a place that has both beaches and mountains. They can decide to split their vacation and spend half the time at the beach and half the time in the mountains. Along these same lines, they can take two long weekends instead of a week and spend one weekend in the mountains and the other weekend at the beach.

Maybe they can agree on a third destination that doesn't have mountains or beaches but will satisfy both of them—perhaps a cabin in the woods or a cruise.

They can flip a coin and allow the winner to choose the vacation location this year, with the understanding that the loser will choose next year's destination.

Another possibility that they may consider: Kelly can go to the beach with her friends while Eric goes to the mountains with his. While not for everyone, separate vacations may be the answer for them.

Had Kelly and Eric each insisted on getting their way, no viable solution could have been found. They both would be placing their individual needs above the needs of the relationship.

Dr. Gary Chapman, author of *The Five Love Languages*, says, "The number one problem in having positive, long-term relationships is selfishness." He says, "We are all egocentric . . . When our self-centeredness becomes selfishness, then we are in for real problems . . . Two selfish people are not going to have a good relationship."

The Solving Circle

Dr. Glasser has developed a way for couples to work together to solve their relationship issues. He calls it Structured Reality Therapy and the Solving Circle.

Most of the time when couples go to a counselor or coach for help with their relationship, they are in a toxic pattern of external control. Couples are spending the vast majority of their time complaining about, criticizing, and blaming each other. They have long ago stopped listening to each other and are locked in a never-ending battle to get their own way—which usually means changing their partner.

The use of the Destructive Relationship Habits creates great strain on their relationship, becoming a downward spiral that is difficult to interrupt unless the couple is willing to change their current behavior by prioritizing their relationship above their individual needs.

Dr. Glasser uses the process of Structured Reality Therapy to work through this problem. It is simply a series of five questions answered alternately by both partners. There are ground rules. The main rule is that while your partner is speaking, your only job is to listen and attempt to understand what your partner is saying from his or her perspective. Should you interrupt your partner, the counselor/coach will remind you of your commitment to allow your partner to speak without interruption. After your partner has had his or her say, then it is your turn to speak.

The first question is, "Are you here because you genuinely want help with your relationship?" This question is designed to weed out those people who are only coming to counseling to appease their significant other. When this is the case, I suggest that the person who is the unhappiest with the relationship seek individual counseling to cope with a partner who is not as invested in the relationship or who doesn't believe a problem exists.

If both people answer yes to the first question, then they are asked the second question, "Whose behavior can you control?" This question is designed to help partners understand that the only person whose behavior they can control is their own. Then they can give up their external control behavior. They can stop focusing on changing their partner and start changing the aspect of their life that they can control . . . their own thoughts and behaviors.

Once the couple agrees that they can't control each other, then they are asked the third question. "Explain what's wrong with your relationship?"

This discussion can become quite lively with multiple interruptions. It is the counselor's job when people interrupt to redirect them by reminding them that they have committed to listen while their partner is speaking and that they will be able to speak when their partner is done.

After each person has listened to the other's complaints about their relationship, the fourth question is, "Now, tell me what's right about your relationship?" This question is designed to get the couple back in touch with the reason they care about salvaging their relationship. There must have been a time when they enjoyed each other's company, had fun with each other, shared a higher level of intimacy and genuinely loved each other. The idea here is to get the partners in touch with these feelings and memories. What's working in their relationship? What do they appreciate about each other?

Then the final question is, "What's one thing you can do all this week that will help your relationship?" This is such an interesting twist. Most relationship counselors ask couples to decide to do something that will satisfy their partner's complaints or desires. This approach is still a subtle form of external control.

By asking the final question of the Structured Reality Therapy as stated above, the counselor is asking each partner to offer a gift of what he or she is willing to do to help the relationship. The overall good of the relationship takes precedence over each individual partner.

While the partner's information is definitely taken into consideration, one partner doesn't necessarily do what the other wants. They have each heard the other's complaints and appreciation of the relationship. The person may choose to stop doing something that his or her partner complained about. Or perhaps the gift will be to begin to do something again that the partner appreciated—something that was right with the relationship. Another possibility may be to create a totally new option based on what the person thinks will most benefit the relationship after taking everything into account. There is no pressure on the individual to choose anything. Neither partner feels coerced into making the change. They both recognize that it is something they want to do for the good of the relationship. Theirs is a gift freely given that's internally motivated out of a strong desire to improve the relationship.

When a couple commits to doing something significant to improve their relationship—and they follow through every day for a week—something magical happens. The dynamics of the relationship improve almost immediately. Couples begin to go out of their way to do positive things to help their relationship.

Once this occurs, Dr. Glasser shares his powerful tool of the Solving Circle with the couple. Any couple can evoke the power of the Solving Circle at any time. All it takes is one partner to be unhappy about something within the relationship, who then asks the other if he or she would be willing to join him or her in the "circle."

Some couples use a literal circle, possibly depicted by an actual physical space, for example a rug or a designated area where they go when working on couple issues. For others, it is a figurative circle which can be used simply to represent a willingness to work through relationship challenges at that time.

When one partner approaches the other with a request to use the circle, one of two things will happen. The partner may say yes, in which case the couple goes through the process of the Solving Circle. Or the partner may say no, in which case the unhappy partner either decides to wait until his or her partner is ready, or decides to take independent action to better manage the situation.

When partners are invited into the Solving Circle and they refuse, what they are saying, in essence, is that they are not ready or willing to place the needs of the relationship above their own needs. They cannot be forced or rushed. The unhappy partners must accept their partner's unwillingness and then decide where to go from there.

However, when partners are willing to use the Solving Circle, then they both get to express what they feel is wrong with the relationship, what they value about the relationship, and they each get to offer a gift to the relationship. This makes it much more likely that the relationship will improve.

Solving Circle Exercise
What to Say to Your Partner

1. "Are you willing to get into the 'Circle' to discuss something that's been bothering me?"
2. "Let me tell you what's wrong from my perspective."
3. "I'd like to hear your side of this issue."
4. "Let me tell you what I appreciate about you and our life together."
5. Since your partner agreed to join the circle, he or she may share anything he or she appreciates as well, but shouldn't feel obligated to do so.
6. "Here is what I'm willing to do about it."

This is a time for the other partner to say what he or she is willing to do to help the relationship. But again, the original partner should not be asking for this, as it is intended to be a freely given gift to your relationship.

This is a tool that can be used for life. All that is required is a commitment to strengthen the relationship above your individual needs.

Stesha and Jamel

Stesha and Jamel were a couple who came to me for coaching. They had been in a five-year, committed relationship but were having difficulty lately. Stesha felt that Jamel was trying to monitor her every move, particularly if she went out with her friends. She felt that she had no freedom and Jamel did not trust her. Jamel, on the other hand, was concerned that Stesha may be seeking a relationship with another man. He was also frustrated because Stesha did not appear to be the person she was in the beginning of their relationship.

When Jamel first met Stesha, she seemed to want what he wanted. She had an entrepreneurial spirit and was going to school. She has since dropped out of school, has had five different jobs, has reenrolled in school for a different major, and now is studying interior design. He can't keep up with her vocation changes and considers her to be irresponsible. When she goes out without him, Jamel is concerned that she may be unwittingly encouraging male attention that could place her in some difficult situations.

When asked what was right with their relationship, both partners said that they genuinely loved the other. They want to spend their lives together. Stesha appreciates that Jamel is a good provider and Jamel appreciates Stesha's creativity.

When it came time to offer their gifts to the relationship, Stesha decided to inform Jamel about decisions she was making, not to win his approval but to help him see that she was transparent and there was nothing for him to be concerned about regarding other men. Jamel agreed to appreciate Stesha's creativity every time he was feeling frustrated with her career changes. Both offered what they were willing to give, made a commitment to doing it, and believed it would serve the higher purpose of their life together.

When they thought about what they could do all this week, Stesha agreed to phone Jamel at least once a day to let him know what her plans were for the day without hiding anything from him. Jamel agreed to find something positive to say to Stesha each day, particularly when he felt critical and judgmental.

After doing this for a week they phoned me to say that they were so much happier and that they didn't think they needed any follow up sessions. They had the tool of the Solving Circle to work through any future issues and had learned some important things about putting their own individual needs on the back burner while prioritizing the needs of the relationship.

Negotiation is a behavior a person has to learn. Most people don't have an aversion to the other person winning, as long as they too can win. However, most of us are unfamiliar with a true win/win/win model and believe it involves compromise—that one or both people have to at least give up some of what they want.

Take the time to learn the art of negotiation. It can be a skill that will assist you with all the relationships in your life, especially your relationship with your significant other.

Chapter Fifteen Summary

1. Taking turns speaking and listening is important to the negotiation process.

2. When it's your turn to listen, your job is to do everything within your power to understand what your partner is saying and to see things from his or her perspective.

3. There is a way to find solutions that result in both you and your partner winning. In the process your relationship becomes stronger, creating win/win/win scenarios.

4. Recognize your part in every relationship challenge and prioritize your relationship over your individual needs.

5. Find something that you can do consistently to improve your relationship. Do it every day regardless of what your partner does or does not do.

Maintenance
The Lesson of the Bonsai

It's good to have money and the things that
money can buy, but it's good, too, to check up
once in a while and make sure that you
haven't lost the things that money can't buy.

—George Lorimer

I have a friend who tells a great story about shopping one day with his adult daughter. While browsing, they both spotted some nice bonsai trees in the plant department and were immediately drawn to them. They both wanted to purchase one for their respective homes. After checking to see if they had the required money necessary for the purchase, both left the store with their bonsai.

They happily went home, positioned their bonsai in just the right place, and went on about their lives. After about two months, both of their bonsai trees had died. My friend uses this story to illustrate how often people may have what it takes to acquire a particular object or person but they do not have the skills and resources necessary to maintain it.

One of my survey respondents wrote, "Dancing is what I did to court my wife. When we got married I didn't have to dance anymore." This is a clear example of acquiring without much thought to maintaining a relationship. This chapter describes how to successfully maintain your relationship with your chosen loved one.

There are many things that couples can do to maintain the happiness and satisfaction within their relationship. Some things, already discussed previously, will only be mentioned here. Other new suggestions will be described in more detail.

Platinum Rule

Remember, Dr. Alessandra's Platinum Rule says: "Do unto others as they would have you do unto them."

People's natural inclination is to give their partner what they themselves desire instead of what their partner would prefer. This is a natural inclination as what we want feels right to us. What a beautiful relationship it would be if, instead, people gave their partner what the partner wants.

Areas of your relationship where you can begin implementing the Platinum Rule follow.

Sex and Romance

As discussed in chapter 10, there is generally a mismatch in this area. Women need romance to feel sexually receptive, while men want sex and aren't particularly inclined to offer romance without a healthy sexual relationship.

The answer here is to once again apply the Platinum Rule. Learn and understand what it is your partner craves and give it to him or her. If you want sex and your partner needs romance to feel sexual, then give her romance. If your partner wants sex and you want to please your partner, stop waiting for romance. Give your partner the sexually exciting relationship he craves.

When you give your partner what he or she wants in this area, you may be surprised at how much of what *you* want will be freely given in return.

Love and Respect

In chapter 11, I mentioned Dr. Eggerichs' book, *Love and Respect*, in which he spoke about a general difference between men and women. He says that in relationships, most men are seeking respect while women are looking for love. In their inclination to apply the Golden Rule instead of the Platinum Rule, most men give their wives respect, while wives give their husbands love. This should be reversed.

The application of the Platinum Rule would eliminate this problem. Women would learn how to let their men know how much they appreciate and respect them; while men would learn how to show their women how much they love and cherish them.

Five Love Languages

Dr. Chapman's book, *The Five Love Languages,* is the book I recommend most to couples who are having difficulty connecting with each other. In it, Chapman lists five different languages people have for experiencing love. If you truly love someone and want him or her to feel loved by you, then you need to speak in his or her "love language."

The five love languages are:

1. Words of affirmation
2. Quality time
3. Receiving gifts
4. Acts of service
5. Physical touch

Each one of these languages is viable. Each person has one that is his or her primary language. People's tendency is to give their partner the thing that helps them feel loved, instead of speaking their partner's primary love language.

For example, when my husband was alive, his love language was acts of service. Mine is quality time. Whenever I wanted my husband to feel I loved him, I would seek him out to spend time with him. When my husband was attempting to show me love, he often did things for me, like fix my car. This was unfortunate. I didn't think he loved me because he hardly ever prioritized quality time with me. He didn't know I loved him because I didn't perform acts of service like making his dinner every night. We were communicating our strong love for each other in a language that was foreign to the other person.

When you want your partner to feel loved by you, you must speak his or her love language, not your own. Once again the application of the Platinum Rule is required. Determine your partner's primary love language and speak the language your partner wants to hear.

Top Ten List

I have created a list of the Top Ten things for men and women to do in their relationships. There is also a Top Ten list of what *not* to do in relationships.

Three things for everyone's list are:

1. Don't go to bed angry.

2. Do trust and respect each other.

3. Don't violate each other's privacy.

Some things specific for women are:

1. Allow your partner time away from you without giving him the third degree.

2. Make love creatively and often. Don't be afraid to initiate lovemaking.

3. Don't compare him to a fictional character in a book, movie, or soap drama and find him lacking.

Some specific things for men are:

1. Continue your courtship even after she's committed to you. Continue to create romance in your relationship.

2. Just listen to your partner without offering advice.

3. Don't take every word she says literally. Women, when upset, tend to speak in absolutes, such as "You NEVER listen to me" when what they really mean is that you aren't listening to them at that time.

Implementing the elements of the Top Ten Lists will help with the maintenance of your relationship. These lists await you at www.Inside-OutEmpowerment.com/HappyCouples/bonusgifts.html.

Treat Your Partner Like Royalty

I was on a trip visiting my mother. One morning I was reading her local newspaper and discovered a poem written by Milli Fitzgerald, a woman who lives in the retirement community of The Villages in Florida. It goes like this:

Never picked up his clothes,
Left the bathroom a mess.
Would finish the cookies,
And never confess.
I'd give him a list,
And he'd swear he'd get to it.
I'll give you three guesses,
The one that would do it.
Of course, I am perfect—
If left on my own.
I should be real happy,
For now I'm alone.
My house looks much neater,
Without really trying.
So why do I spend my time
Lonely and crying?
I think of the good times;
Oh yes, there were plenty!
That my blessings were many.
If given a chance to live it again,
I would so gladly
Pick up after him!

If you want to engage in positive maintenance behavior, remembering the words of this poem will help. If you treat your partner as if today could be either of your last days on Earth, then you will treat each other like royalty. Why is this so difficult?

Everyday we tend to allow petty annoyances to become our focus. We would never say or do anything hurtful if we knew it would be our partner's last day on Earth.

When you have a negative thought directed at your partner, stop a moment and ask yourself, "Would I even care about this if I knew that either my partner or I wouldn't be here tomorrow"? If the answer is no, change the thought by finding something to appreciate instead.

The Last Breath

None of us know when we will be taking our last breath. You can continue to live your life as if you and everyone you care about will live forever. Or you can start prioritizing your time so that if you don't open your eyes tomorrow, you will be satisfied with the way you spent your time today.

I am not suggesting that you live your life irresponsibly, quit your job, and spend your life's savings on a trip around the world. What I am suggesting is that you get and stay "right" with the important people in your life, especially your life partner. Has a disagreement kept you from showing kindness or affection to your partner? What if he or she were gone? Do you put off spending time with your loved one, thinking that there will always be time tomorrow or next week? What if there is no tomorrow? Do you go through your day exhausting yourself doing things that everyone else wants you to do without thought to keeping yourself strong so you can be here tomorrow?

Take control of your time. Prioritize. What would you change if today were your last day? Spend time with those you love. Tell your loved ones you love them. Do something for yourself. Forgive past hurts. Focus your energy on what's important in the grand scheme of things.

Give Attention to the Little Things

Pay attention to the positive things. Everyday your loved one does things which you can appreciate. He or she may go to work to earn money for the household. Maybe your partner stayed out of your way so you could get something accomplished. Maybe he or she began your day with a warm greeting. Pay attention to the little things. Everyday provides these opportunities.

When you are frustrated with your partner, you wear your "frustration lenses," noticing only the things that frustrate or annoy you. When you wear your "appreciation lenses," you can find an amazing number of things to appreciate. As a widow, this may come easier for me since I've experienced first-hand how tenuous life can be. I appreciate that my partner wakes up each morning. I love that he cooks for me. I appreciate how he is protective of me. He is very generous. He challenges me so I can think things through before I deliver information to an audience. There is so very much to appreciate!

As you read this, you may think I've got an exceptional man. While that is true, if I were to switch to my frustration lenses, I would be describing a very different person. Nothing has changed. He still is the same person, doing the things he does from day to day. What has changed is the way I see him.

Which lenses do you wear most days? You can totally transform your partner by changing your perspective.

Past Pain and Self-Sabotage

Dr. Gray mentions the common cycle of ups and downs in relationships. One day you feel madly in love with each other and the next day you can't stand the sight of each other. Why does this happen?

Dr. Gray theorizes that experiencing the positive, comfortable feeling of love can bring up old unresolved feelings. "One day we are feeling loved, and the next day we are suddenly afraid to trust love."

Whenever we are experiencing more love in our life, whether it is self-love or the love of another, old repressed feelings from the past can surface and interfere with the positive feelings we are experiencing.

Dr. Gray believes it is the safe haven of feeling love that allows these unresolved feelings to surface, seeking healing in the current situation. When you can recognize what is happening, then you can make significant progress toward healing past relationship pain. However, if you use these scary, unresolved feelings to lash out at your partner, then you will continue to repeat the patterns of your past, condemning yourself to reliving similar experiences.

Dr. Hendricks theorizes that this pattern happens for a similar but slightly different reason. He sees it as an Upper Limit Problem. Whenever we begin to experience deeper levels of intimacy with our partner, we exceed the "set point" of what we believe is possible and we will engage in mostly subconscious sabotaging behavior. We will become jealous, accusatory, and lash out at our loved one, feeling completely justified.

If you are in a loving relationship, it is helpful to be aware that when your partner lashes out at you in anger, hurt, and frustration, most of the time it has very little to do with you or your character. Predominantly, it is intimately connected to something happening within your partner's psyche. Try to remember that it isn't really about you and don't take it personally.

It is critical during these times to remain confident in who you are, to not get defensive, and to support your significant other in discovering what is really happening in the present situation.

Keeping Score

Another behavior that isn't good for the maintenance of relationships is expecting something in return whenever you give something to your partner. It isn't truly a gift when there are strings attached.

When you love someone, it is natural to want to do things for that person. In a loving relationship, partners do things for each other on a regular basis. However, when you give, are you truly giving from your heart or are there strings attached?

People have asked me after someone they were dating breaks up with them: "Do you think it is wrong of me to want to get _____ back?" And of course the blank involves some kind of gift that they gave the person. Unless the gift was an engagement ring, I don't believe gifts should be returned. Once you give a gift to someone, you no longer have claim to that gift. Ownership has been transferred.

There are people who keep a running tally in their heads of everything they ever did for their partner. The subject will never come up as long as the relationship remains reciprocal. But if the one keeping track begins to notice that the other person isn't giving as much, then the first person will start feeling unappreciated, listing everything he or she has done for the other person, and how ungrateful that has been.

"I spent this much on our vacation." "I paid for her to go here and there." "I bought him this and that." There is no genuine spirit of giving when this happens. It seems that the gifts were meant to obligate the other. Giving should be for the simple joy and pleasure of giving. It isn't about doing something for someone else in the hopes that you will get something in return. A gift is a gift.

In addition to material objects, you can also give of your time and energy. Did you ever feel short-changed in the amount you give to a relationship? Then stop giving. Don't keep giving to the point where you begin to look at the other person with resentment. Decide how much you are willing to invest in the relationship and create your own boundaries. That way, if a relationship ends, you won't have to feel as if you gave too much and were cheated.

Give with a willing heart and you will be rewarded with the good feeling that comes from giving. When you want or expect something in return, it detracts from the pure purpose of the gift.

If your relationship ends, don't start adding up the score to figure out who owes whom more. Simply relish the feelings you had during the relationship and be grateful for learning that this isn't the right person for you. Now you are free to explore other relationships until you find a more compatible partner.

Date Night

One of the things that works to keep relationships alive is spending quality time with each other. In this information age, it is becoming increasingly difficult to carve out the necessary time to nurture our relationships. What with long work hours, helping kids with their homework, transporting them around to their extracurricular activities, making dinner, cleaning up, and going through the bedtime routine, what time is left?

Unless you orchestrate the time for your relationship, other less important things will crowd in and take up all your precious time. Pick a night that will be "date night" with your partner and make a game out of being as creative as you can be. Try to see how many things you can do without spending money. Some examples include: sitting outside on the deck on a warm summer's night looking at the stars, watching a movie, preparing a meal together, going for a ride, having a picnic by a lake— and don't forget good, old-fashioned intimacy, romance, and sex. When you prioritize spending quality time with the person you love, it sends a very clear message to your partner that he or she is important to you.

If you are looking for some suggestions of things to do with your partner that don't cost a lot of money, I've compiled a list for you at www.InsideOutEmpowerment.com/HappyCouples/bonusgifts.html, entitled, *52 Low or No Cost Things to Do on a Date*.

It is so easy to get caught up in the hustle and bustle, the drama and trauma of life, that you consequently take your loved ones for granted. You trust that they will always be there. After all, isn't it enough that you come home every night, take care of the household chores, pay the bills, are faithful, don't use drugs or alcohol, etc.?

While these things are important, it is also critical to allocate special one-on-one time with your significant other. You don't answer telephones; you don't check emails; you simply don't allow other things to take priority. During this agreed upon time, spending quality time with your loved one is all that matters.

Karen and Jack

One couple who took my survey was joking about the importance of date night. Really, this couple epitomizes the importance of humor in relationships. When asked what they do to nurture their relationship, they told me that they have date night every Wednesday night. Karen described this as a romantic drive. Jack, on the other hand, said, "Yes, Thursday is garbage day. So every Wednesday night, we load the garbage in our SUV and drive the length of our two-mile driveway to put the garbage out."

Seriously, making time for one another to do something enjoyable together, without the children, is a great way to maintain romance in your relationship. Remember that this is meant to be a pleasure, a reward, a treat. Do not allow scheduling date night to become another chore. That would take the pleasure right out of it.

Sometimes romance goes out of relationships because people allow their lives to become so busy and full that there is no time left for their partner. When they do get together, both people are so exhausted and stressed that it seems like sex is just one more thing on the "to do list." Do your relationship a favor and schedule at least one date night a week that is sacred, just for you and your partner. Get back in touch with each other and don't let anything—I mean anything—get in your way. You won't be sorry.

The main point is not to see how kinky you can get. The idea is to keep your relationship alive by making time together a priority. It is important that you find things to do as a couple that you both enjoy. If you have vastly different interests, then you can take turns and each agree to happily participate in the activity chosen by the one whose turn it is that week.

As long as you make a habit of making your relationship a priority and allocating time each week to rejuvenate the feelings that attracted you in the first place, you stand a good chance of staying together for the long haul.

Don't allow insidious boredom to enter into your relationship through the back door. This is what frequently happens when you are busy placing other things ahead of your time for each other. You know what I mean—the job, the kids, your friend in crisis, etc. There will always be competing interests for the time you've set aside for each other.

Other than a natural disaster, threat of death, or major crisis, do not allow your time together to be invaded by any outside forces. Make sure to create opportunities to do things together without outside influence. With more than 50% of today's marriages ending in divorce, make this small investment in the longevity of your relationship. You have nothing to lose and everything to gain.

Love As A Way of Life

Dr. Chapman wrote a book entitled, *Love as a Way of Life*. In it he challenges the reader to imagine what it would be like if everyone practiced the "Seven Keys to Transforming Every Aspect of Your Life." The seven keys are: kindness, patience, forgiveness, courtesy, humility, generosity, and honesty. Sometimes we are better able to practice these traits with strangers. Imagine what would happen if you used them with those you love and especially with yourself? When you love yourself enough to practice these behaviors with yourself, it can't help but improve your relationship with your significant other. Then, consciously engage in the Seven Keys with your partner and see how you can transform your relationship into Heaven on Earth.

Chapter Sixteen Summary

1. Our relationships require constant nurturing to thrive. They may survive if we forget to feed them once in a while. But in order to thrive, we need to constantly pay attention to what's important.

2. Remember to employ the Platinum Rule in all things.

3. Don't allow sex and romance to die.

4. Learn and speak your partner's love language.

5. Treat your partner as if today could be either one of your last days on Earth.

6. Appreciate and mention the little things each of you do.

7. When your partner lashes out at you, don't take it personally.

8. Schedule a regular date night.

There Are No Secrets
Anything Goes

We can never judge the lives of others, because each person
knows only their own pain and renunciation.
It's one thing to feel that you are on the right path,
but it's another to think that yours is the only path.

—Paulo Coelho

This chapter explores what relationship experts say can help build strong, healthy relationships, as well as what happy couples report helps their relationships. This chapter also discusses establishing healthy boundaries for your relationship and makes a case for how only you and your partner can determine what will work best for your relationship.

When I interviewed the professional relationship experts, I wanted to find out what they thought were the three most important things individuals could do to nurture their relationships. While they didn't all have three things to say, they did have excellent advice on how to create and maintain healthy relationships.

What the Professionals Say

What can couples do to nurture their relationship with each other?

Dr. Gary Chapman says:

1. Create a time for daily sharing, to verbally connect with each other.
2. Learn each other's love language.
3. Learn how to listen empathetically—to understand not only what your partner is saying but also what he or she is feeling.

Dr. Karen Kan says:

1. Get expert relationship help, ideally *before* problems arise.
2. Check in on the health and growth of the relationship at least monthly.
3. Make it a habit to appreciate each other daily—either verbally, with love notes, or with physical affection.

Dr. Harville Hendrix says:

1. Create emotional safety.
2. Live authentically and vulnerably.

Arielle Ford says:

Create a clear daily intention to love, honor, and cherish each other—and keep choosing it over and over again.

Drs. Gay and Katie Hendricks sum up their advice in their *Conscious Living and Loving Initiative* found at www.hendricks.com/conscious_initiative:

1. Speak honestly, rather than concealing the truth.
2. Take healthy responsibility, wondering rather than blaming others.
3. Express appreciation, rather than criticize.

What Happy Couples Report

When I was surveying satisfied, happy couples, I expected to find some commonalities among them. In general, there were four trends I found.

First, 83% of survey respondents said they have not had sexual relationships outside their committed relationship. Commitment and monogamy seem to be factors in maintaining healthy relationships.

Second, 25% reported having a spiritual component to their relationship—a Higher Power to which they felt accountable. In addition, 34% spoke of putting the needs of their partner and their relationship above their own individual needs as crucial to their success. Ms. Ford says that the relationship must come first. Dr. Hendrix says, "The relationship is foundational and is the priority." Having something more important than your own individual interests seems to be a common foundation to happiness in relationships.

Third, 29% of respondents reported that they accept their partners just the way they are. When asked what three things respondents would change about their partner, 36% said absolutely nothing. Of those who did list things they would like to change, 32% spoke of things that would benefit their partner or their overall relationship. For example, one said, "I wish he'd stop smoking so he would be healthier." Another said, "I wish she'd be more outgoing so she could meet more people." An overall acceptance of one's partner just as he or she is seems to be another important factor in relationship success.

Fourth, the couples who reported being happy and satisfied place high value on effective communication and the use of the seven Healthy Relationship Habits. Effective communication was listed as the #1 ingredient to a happy relationship by 59% of those who took my survey.

Beyond these four trends, the patterns cease to exist. For some couples sexual compatibility was important. Others prioritized financial concerns. Some couples found that having a partner with whom they were matched intellectually was important. Others found that having compatibility with outside relationships was most important: seeing eye-to-eye on parenting, liking each other's parents or children from previous relationships, having friends in common, and respecting their partner's friendships which don't include them. The conclusion is that anything goes in relationships provided it works for the two people involved.

Challenges and Opportunities

Challenges typically come in the form of differences, many of which were discussed in chapter 14. Some of the differences reported were differences in culture, religion, age, and political views.

Ms. Ford says that when people come from similar backgrounds, the learning curve is shorter. However, differences can work in relationships when a couple chooses to make them work.

Dr. Kan says that differences can be enriching, as well as challenging. We attract people who are our mirrors in order to help us heal our personal wounds. What annoys us in another, is often a trait that we cannot accept in ourselves. Differences are there to encourage us to stretch out of our comfort zone and it is this "stretching" which helps us grow in intimacy and connection.

Dr. Chapman says that challenges in relationships come from differences. A couple has to face them and decide how to resolve them with an attitude of love.

When couples can view their differences as opportunities to learn, stretch from their comfort zones, and grow in understanding, differences can enhance each individual and strengthen the couple.

Boundaries

Another challenge that can sometimes occur is interference from people who are outside the primary relationship. This interference can come from children, parents, well-intentioned friends, not-so-well-intentioned friends, acquaintances, and strangers.

Everyone has an opinion and sometimes these opinions will extend to your behavior or character, your partner's behavior or character, or your relationship in general. People often express their opinions, either directly to you or behind your back. Unfortunately, they can pass judgment on something about your relationship, creating fear and doubt when it wasn't there before.

Stranger Danger: Sometimes this interference will be completely unsolicited. You might be a tall female dating a shorter man, and while you are out dancing you hear someone else on the dance floor say, "Don't they look ridiculous together?" You may be in an interracial relationship and hear a Black woman say, "See, once a brother makes it, he goes for the White girls." You and your partner may agree on your parenting approach but an outsider may comment on it. For example, you are at a grocery store and your child refuses to listen. You pick him up and leave the store without purchasing your groceries. As you are leaving, you hear someone say, "That's what's wrong with kids today. There is no discipline."

These are all examples of strangers expressing their unsolicited opinions about things that are working well for you. You hear their comments and begin to doubt yourself and your choices.

When comments come from people you don't know, it is unlikely that they will be helpful to your relationship. This is a time for you to consider the source and move on. Establish impenetrable boundaries for strangers. Do not allow what others say to interfere with your relationship satisfaction. Don't let them in. They do not have your best interest at heart. They don't even know you. They are responding to their own emotional baggage and limitations. Don't allow their issues to become yours.

Unsolicited Friend and Family Advice: Sometimes family and friends will offer unsolicited advice. You can be happy in your relationship, but people close to you may see things that they think are not right. People who care about you can sometimes see things in your relationship that you don't notice. Is it that they can see things more clearly because they aren't in it? Sometimes. Is it because they see things that aren't really there for you? Sometimes. People can look at your relationship and see things that would never work for them but are no problem for you.

In this situation, you need to have flexible boundaries. You need to stop those who would criticize your relationship and at the same time listen to see if there is any validity to what they are saying. This is what flexible boundaries mean.

You have an internal mechanism that let's you know if you are getting what you want from your relationship. When you aren't getting what you want, you feel unsettled or worse. When you are getting what you want, you feel happy.

Tim and Cindy

Tim is a construction worker, whose job is very physically demanding. Cindy is a school teacher, whose job requires more mental concentration. When they get home at the end of their day, Tim likes to relax and help their children with homework. Cindy cooks dinner and does household chores.

Cindy's sister, Laurie, thinks it is unfair that Cindy has to work all day and come home to make dinner and do the household chores every night. She thinks Tim needs to be more helpful around the house. However Cindy is perfectly fine with the arrangement because Tim handles the homework, which is something Cindy deals with all day and doesn't want to do when she gets home.

In this case, Cindy might want to consider what her sister is saying. She may try to see the situation from Laurie's position. She recognizes that Laurie is coming from a protective place and understands her point of view. She can even appreciate Laurie looking out for her, even though she disagrees with Laurie's perspective.

Cindy is flexible enough to consider Laurie's comment but has good boundaries so that she does not accept Laurie's perspective as her own. If she did, she might start an argument with Tim about his doing more around the house when this isn't really an issue in their relationship.

Getting information from others can be helpful but remember, people can only see things from their perspective. No one knows better than you what is best for you.

Solicited Advice: There are times when we actually ask for the advice of others. There will be times when you are unsure about your relationship and may want to talk with someone you trust. However, every time you and your partner have a disagreement and you bring a third party into it, you set yourself up to get advice. It's human nature to want to fix problems. When you talk to a friend or family member about concerns you are having within your relationship, you open up your boundaries.

When you are experiencing conflict in your relationship, it is natural to seek support from those who care about you. However you seldom bring others into the situation to understand your partner better. Usually, you tell others so they can validate your feeling of being right and judge your partner wrong.

This works well in the short-term. You feel better about your position and feel justified in your anger toward your partner. However, it is almost always destructive in the long run.

When you are experiencing a problem with your partner that is unresolved and you share the intimate details of the situation with others, you are not respecting your partner's privacy. You are sharing personal things with other people without having your partner's permission. This may create additional problems for your relationship.

Another problem that can be created when soliciting others' advice is that your one-sided account of the situation can color others' opinions about your partner. If every time you and your partner disagree, you call your mother or your best friend to talk about it, they will probably judge your partner and alter their interactions with him or her. Long after you have worked out your disagreements, your family and friends may be responding negatively toward your partner.

It is most helpful when you are unsure about your relationship to speak directly to your partner. This honors your partner by not sharing personal information with others outside your relationship. There are some who adamantly object to having their intimate relationship details shared with others, particularly if it affects others' opinions of them.

It is important to honor your partner by deciding together if and when you share your relationship issues with others. This is not to say that you can't ask opinions from people you trust as long as you consider what is said objectively. Having permeable boundaries around your relationship provides the best of both worlds. You can ask others' opinions, filtering them for truth as you see it, but not allowing others to dictate what you and your partner will do within the sanctity of your relationship.

No Judgments

When I was seeking respondents for my survey, I placed an ad in the American Counseling Association's publication, *Counseling Today*, a magazine for therapists. Several couples responded to my ad and were willing to help; one of them was Sam and Kelly. As a counselor who has worked in prisons, mental health facilities, and a special needs foster care agency, I thought there was nothing left that could surprise me. However, this couples' story surprised me and it is a clear indication that no one can dictate what works in relationships except for the two people who are in it. What follows is the account Sam and Kelly provided.

Sam/Samantha and Kelly

Sam and Kelly lived in a Midwestern state when they got married. They were committed and happy in their relationship and from the beginning agreed to an open marriage, one in which either partner could engage in sexual activity with outside partners without fear of reprisal from the other. For years, this is what worked for them.

After 12 years of marriage, Sam was diagnosed with testicular cancer. At the time, his doctor told him that the best odds for a total cure would be his submitting to a sex change operation. After much consideration, discussion, and counseling, Sam underwent the drastic procedure and has since received a clean bill of health. He became Samantha, and Samantha and Kelly began the next phase of their marriage as a lesbian couple.

They enjoy an active sex life. With Samantha's blessing, Kelly has an outside heterosexual relationship with a man to satisfy her desire for intercourse. Kelly's sexual partner is also married and has an open marriage with his wife. Everyone is honest and above board. No one gets hurt.

Samantha said, "We realized that being together, even in a somewhat new form, was better than being apart or my being dead. . . . We both real-

ized that body parts were not as important as the soul of the person. . . .
We make good money, love our jobs, travel, have friends, a nice house, two
vehicles, time shares in Mexico, and other trappings. We discuss everything.
I worry more about money; she worries more about the laundry."

Kelly admitted, "I really was not sure I wanted to stay in the relationship
until she actually moved away from me to take another job. After a period
of time, I knew that this person is the one I want to be with—to face the
world with—the one that I am good with and that is good with me . . . I
wasn't sure that I could deal with the pressure of society thinking I was a
lesbian when in reality I wasn't. It takes a while to change your internal
perception. Frankly now I don't care what society thinks. I am with the
person I love. I'm okay with the label bi-sexual. I doubt I will ever see
myself as a lesbian regardless of what the outside of our relationship looks
like to others."

From the outside looking in, you may have several value judgments
about this relationship. You certainly have the right to refrain from engaging in a similar arrangement yourself. However, if two people are happy
and satisfied in their relationship, what right does anyone have from the
outside to criticize that couple? Even if your objection is religious, most
religions with which I'm familiar encourage followers not to judge. Judgment is the job of the Higher Power.

How you work on your relationship challenges should be based upon
your individual and collective needs, wants, missions, and visions. Your
individual desires should be used to craft your relationship direction
together. You, and you alone, can determine what will work for you as a
couple.

Chapter Seventeen Summary

1. Professionals have great advice for couples who want to nurture their relationship.

2. Happy couples have a few things in common:

   a. Monogamy

   b. Making either a Higher Power or their relationship a priority over their individual wants and needs

   c. An acceptance of who their partner is without trying to change him or her

   d. The use of effective communication

3. Differences can create challenge or growth.

4. Permeable boundaries around the partnership seem to provide the best approach when dealing with the outside world.

All Physical Relationships End
What Is Your Lesson and/or Gift?

Don't cry because it's over; smile because it happened.

—Dr. Seuss

All Physical Relationships Will End

So often we can get caught up in wanting our relationships to last "forever," forgetting that there are never any forever guarantees. We lose loved ones due to death, divorce, distance, or personal decision. No matter how the end occurs, it is painful. When you love someone, you want him or her to always be in your life.

A wise person once said, "Some people come into our lives for a reason, some for a season, and some for a lifetime." The mistake we make is trying to turn a "reason" or a "season" person into a "lifetime" person. This will not work.

When you adopt total trust in a Higher Power and you realize that everything happens according to a plan greater than your own narrow view of the world, then you know that all things that happen are meant to be.

Grief: Resisting Reality

Starting over after the loss of a loved one is a monumental task that feels overwhelming at times. Similar rebuilding occurs whether the loss is due to the death, divorce, distance, or decision of a loved one.

In her book, *On Death and Dying,* Elizabeth Kublar-Ross describes the five stages of grief people go through:

1. Denial and isolation
2. Anger
3. Bargaining
4. Depression
5. Acceptance

People go through these stages when they experience not just death, but other major losses such as divorce. There is no "right" way to experience these stages. You will go through them at your own pace. You may skip some and revisit others. Whatever happens, it is *your* path and no one else's.

You may be in the anger phase, then jump to depression, and then go back to denial. There is no rhyme or reason—only what feels right for each individual at the time. No one can predict how long a phase will last. If you are grieving and some well-meaning people suggest that you shouldn't be feeling what you are feeling, kindly thank them for their concern but know that you are exactly where you need to be. However, if you are the one who starts thinking, "I should be over this by now," then it may be time to move beyond your grief.

If a devastating loss has happened to you, you already know about the five stages. Everything seems fine. You are happy. You have a partner in your life who meets most of your needs. You depend on that person. You imagine your future together. You take for granted that you will always be together. Then something happens that is totally out of your control and your world is shattered.

First comes the shock of the loss and a denial that it has happened, particularly if there was no warning. You had hopes and dreams of the future that included your loved one and suddenly he or she is not there. How will you cope? How can you go on?

But go on you must and you will. Oftentimes your first step is to attempt to regain what you lost. This is impossible if your loved one died but that doesn't stop you from trying. Much of what people go through in their grieving process involves their attempt to keep their loved one alive and well—even if it's only in their mind. So, you may do things such as go over the memories, look through picture albums, listen to music that reminds you of your lost relationship, talk about your loved one to everyone who will listen, think about him or her every minute, and even speak to him or her out loud.

It can be even more challenging if your loved one didn't die but has chosen to walk out of your life. In this case, you not only have to get over the shock of the loss but also cope with the feelings of rejection. These feelings are certainly experienced in divorce and even dating situations.

In their best attempt to get their loved one back, people engage in all the behaviors that someone who has lost their partner to death would. But in addition, they may beg their partners to come back, follow their loved ones around, try to get their friends to intervene on their behalf, and a host of other maladaptive behaviors.

All behavior is purposeful—meaning it is your best attempt to get something you want so you can meet one or more of your needs. Grief is no exception.

What could you possibly be trying to get by grieving? Most people would say that they don't have a choice. When someone you love dies, you have to grieve. It is natural that you will miss your loved one's presence in your life but it isn't inevitable that you *have* to grieve, not in the way most people think of grieving.

I believe that by grieving people are trying to get back the person who died. When you grieve, it is your best attempt to keep that person alive, at least in your perception. You know that they no longer exist in your day-to-day reality. But continuing to think about them, pining for them, and grieving their absence, keeps the thought of that person active in your imagination. It feels better to you than the total void or absence of the other person.

Another possible advantage of grief is that it shows others just how much you loved the person who is gone. Grief says, "See what a good

_____ I was." Fill in the blank with husband, wife, boyfriend, girlfriend, mother, father, sister, brother, etc. (This is not to say that people are being consciously manipulative in their grief.)

Grief is also instrumental in getting you the support you need from others during your time of bereavement. People do things for you that you would normally be expected to do yourself. Of course a grieving person does not wake up and "decide" to grieve so that someone will stop by the house with a meal. These are not conscious decisions but they are still potential advantages of grief.

If you are grieving, or you are involved in the life of someone who is grieving, please don't judge yourself or them. Understand that all behavior is purposeful and the grieving person is getting something out of what they are doing. When they become conscious that there is a choice, then they can decide which of the three choices they want to make: leave it; change it; or accept it.

Clarify Your Goal

Before we talk about what to do, it is important to really examine and define what you want. Most people who have lost their partner want him or her back. They want to pinch themselves in the hope that they were just having a nightmare. They want their partner to love them again.

Without taking a good look at what you want, you tend to start behaving unconsciously. You want your life back so you start engaging in activities to try to change the other person's mind. You cry; you rage; you get depressed; and sometimes in desperation, you might even engage in stalking behavior.

Your partner has told you that the relationship is over. He is not interested in continuing your life together. Your partner isn't in love with you anymore, and that is completely unacceptable to you. You think that your loved one is losing his mind. He might be having a midlife crisis. Your mind kicks into denial. You simply don't believe it.

You call your friends, trying to get them on your side to validate whatever it is you are thinking. In sheer desperation, you start to spy on your loved one. You drive by where he works. You make unwanted phone calls, begging him to come back and give you one more chance. You start approaching his family and friends hoping to gain the insight you lack.

All of this is understandable when you behave without having your goal in mind. If you don't understand that your goal is to reinstate the relationship, then your behavior seems justified. However, when you clearly define your goal, then you can ask yourself the question, "Are the behaviors I am engaging in helping me bring this person back into my life?"

When you honestly look at the situation, you have to admit that what you are doing is more likely pushing your loved one away. Once you recognize this, you need to switch out of your emotional mode and move into a more logical, intellectual mode.

You need to understand a little about relationship dynamics. Until a couple truly moves into an area of mature love and relationship commitment, they tend to go through cycles. One partner withdraws and the other person moves closer in an attempt to fill the gap created by the withdrawal. In so doing, the person attempting to fill the gap often crowds and smothers his or her partner, thus increasing the likelihood of being rejected. It's a vicious cycle.

What can be done to break the cycle? You must honor your partner in your relationship, while at the same time honoring yourself. You do not have the right to get your own needs met at the expense of your partner's needs. When a relationship is not meeting the needs of both individuals, sometimes one or both people decide it's time to end it.

A problem occurs if you don't want the relationship to end and your partner does. What can you do? The first thing to always ask yourself is, "Whose behavior can I control?" If your partner has decided to end the relationship, is there really anything you can do to stop him? Maybe, and that's a big maybe, you can make him feel so guilty that he will return to you. However, do you want to create a relationship built on a foundation of guilt?

You must honor your partner's wishes to end a relationship gracefully, if your goal is to maintain some type of relationship with him in the future. You may be able to salvage a friendship this way. It's even possible that down the road, your partner may want to return to you once he realizes that you respected him enough to let him go gracefully. However, don't let this be the reason you do so because then if he doesn't come back, you may reengage in some crazy-making behaviors.

You have a right to a fulfilling, satisfying relationship. However, this may not be possible with the partner who left. Hold on to your vision of the future—your dream of happily ever after. Allow yourself the flexibility to imagine a fulfilling relationship with a different partner in your life. After all, isn't part of your vision to be in relationship with someone who loves you as much as you love him? Then your current relationship is not the answer.

Let your partner go gracefully with the knowledge that you are better off for the time you spent in the relationship. It met your needs for as long as it existed and now you are on to bigger and better things. You have been freed to continue your search for a more compatible partner.

Attempting to hold on to someone who is already gone only causes suffering and heartache. Remember that an ending is always a beginning. You simply have to reframe your relationship. When a relationship ends, don't look to place blame. Understand that it has run its course. You have been shown the important lessons and now this person must leave your life to allow the next phase to begin. Embrace it and learn from it.

And remember the quote by Dr. Seuss, "Don't cry because it's over; smile because it happened."

Choices: Change It, Accept It, or Leave It

In chapter 4, we discussed how there are always at least three choices in every situation: change it, accept it, or leave it.

With death, you may wonder how someone is going to "leave it." Well, some possible ways would be major denial of the loss, suicide, drugs and/ or alcohol abuse, or sinking deep into mental illness.

When a loved one dies, people may continue grieving as their best attempt to get the person back. This might look like constant trips to the cemetery, frequent conversations with the deceased, refusing to believe that he or she is truly gone, and/or constantly talking about the one who's gone. There are many things people can do in an attempt to change the reality of the death.

If and when you come to accept it, you can experience some measure of peace and rejoin the living. A healthy step in this process is finding a way to somehow maintain that person's presence in your life in a healthy way. This is a very individual process and you will find a way that works for you.

Most people have seen the movie, *Meet the Parents*. In it, Robert De Nero's character kept the ashes of his mother in an urn on his mantle. Many people do this with the cremated remains of their loved ones. Others place some ashes in a necklace and wear it around their neck. Some will set up scholarships or memorials. When my husband died, his family and I created a wrestling scholarship fund for a local high school wrestler. When my friend lost her eight year-old son, she had the Houston zoo name their frog exhibit after him!

There are all kinds of creative ways to responsibly maintain the person's presence. There is no wrong way. Whatever brings comfort to you without interfering with the rest of your life should be supported by those around you—even if it makes them uncomfortable.

When you choose acceptance, you can begin assimilating back into your life and the lives of those around you. But it may not happen overnight. Exercise patience and loving understanding with yourself as you begin your journey back from grief.

On the other hand, some people deal with death by appearing not to grieve at all. There may be many explanations for this behavior. They may be very private and won't grieve in front of others. Or perhaps they are trying to be strong for everyone else. They may be criticized by some for not grieving enough.

This is not the time for you to be worried about what others think of your decisions. It's important for you to find out what works for you.

Finding the Lesson and/or the Gift

Each person who crosses your path in an intimate way is someone from whom you have a lesson to learn. Value the lesson and when the time is right, allow that person to exit your life. Stop trying to hold on to someone who is ready to move down the road without you.

My Story

My husband passed away eleven years ago. He was only 37 years old. We loved each other very much and had two boys who were teenagers at the time. While his death was the darkest period in my life, I can see some advantages—after much time, space, and distance from that event.

One of the first positives was that I actually had the opportunity to say goodbye. My husband's entire family had the opportunity to say the things they wanted to say to him to bring closure to their relationships. Many people do not have that opportunity when loved ones are taken away suddenly.

Secondly, I did not live in an area of the country that I liked. I lived where he lived. Five years later I moved to Chicago, a place I truly love.

Thirdly, I got to raise my boys alone—which was both bad news and good news. Raising them alone was a lot of hard work and the most challenging test of my life. However, going through that experience, definitely made me a stronger person, equipping me with the fortitude I need in my life right now while I am building my business.

A fourth benefit is that when my husband learned that he was sick, he stopped working. He didn't stop because he was too sick. He stopped because there was some research link between his type of leukemia and the chemical benzene—something he worked with at his job. Prior to his illness, my husband was a workaholic. Once diagnosed, he began to spend lots of quality time with our children. He coached soccer; he coached Little League; he taught our boys how to work on cars; and he spent long hours with them hunting and fishing. This would not have happened had he lived to be a hundred years old with his workaholic behavior.

Finally, I am currently in a nourishing relationship with a wonderful man. We are extremely compatible, supporting and celebrating each other. This is not an experience I would have had if my husband were still alive.

Several mechanics who knew my husband now wear latex gloves while working on engines. My husband's illness and their subsequent precautions might just save their lives.

And there was even an advantage for my husband's best friend from high school. He was gay but knew that my husband wouldn't accept him as a homosexual. He came out after my husband was gone. I wonder if he would still be in the closet today if my husband had lived.

If I am able to find gifts in my husband's death, you too can find the benefit in the loss of your relationship. It merely involves putting on the proper lenses that will allow you to see it. In science, you don't see protons (positive charges) without electrons (negative charges). Similarly, you won't have a devastating event in your life without it also carrying some benefits. The key is to look for the positive instead of the negative. Finding the benefits will allow you to heal and move on.

One of the first steps in healing your grief is to reach out to those who love you. When someone you love leaves you, a huge void is created in your life. Some people try to fill this void with drugs or alcohol, but this only results in a temporary reprieve from the pain. Others seek meaningless encounters confusing sex with love. However this only postpones the inevitable—feeling the pain of their lost love. People who jump into a relationship too quickly are likely to end up in a vicious cycle of never finding real love.

If love is what you lost, then the only thing that will help you truly feel better is more love. You must replace love with love. Reach out to friends, family, and co-workers—anyone who will fill some of the gap left by your loved one. It's not the same, it's not what you are really craving, but it will help ease, and eventually heal the pain.

When the pain starts to heal, you will gain strength and can start rebuilding your life. You can go on. You can laugh again. And yes, you can love again.

Love has many forms. You may develop another relationship in time. You may find a cause that you love. You may "adopt" a neighborhood child. You may find or create work you love. You may get a pet that you can love unconditionally. You may become involved (but hopefully not over-involved) in the lives of your children. Whatever form love takes, it will begin to fill the void that was left from the relationship you lost.

If you feel as if your life is over, you are truly wasting the gift of life that you have been given. There is only one you. You have something unique to offer the rest of us. Please don't keep it hidden, lost in your grief. Do not climb in the grave with your loved one. It is not your time. Find someone less fortunate than you, and do something for them without expecting anything in return. You'll be surprised what that does to elevate your mood.

In every ending, there is possibility and potential. When you lose someone you love, give thanks for the time you were granted and look to the future for something even better.

Chapter Eighteen Summary

1. Unless both of you die simultaneously, your "forever" relationship will end, leaving one of you alone.

2. There are five stages of grief that most people travel through: denial, anger, bargaining, depression, and acceptance.

3. Most human suffering comes from an inability to accept circumstances and situations the way they are. We attempt to change things that cannot be changed.

4. Grief can serve many purposes. Some will be helpful; others will not be.

5. "Don't cry because it's over; smile because it happened."

6. There are always three options in a relationship: you can change it, accept it, or leave it.

7. When your relationship ends and it wasn't by your choice, look for the lesson and/or the gift. If you look, you will find it.

Appendix One

InsideOut Empowerment Resources
Programs to Help You Improve the Relationships with the Important People in Your Lives, Including Yourself, at Home and at Work

Now that you know how to improve your relationship with your significant other and yourself, you may want some additional support to stay on the path. And you may have other relationships you want to improve. To help you get there faster, I created the following programs that provide you with even greater support than you can get from a book by itself.

InsideOut Empowerment **Seminars**
In the InsideOut Empowerment Seminar, I will teach you the foundational principles of how to transform your life by putting your energy into that over which you have power and control—YOU! You will learn to implement the Healthy Relationship Habits, while reducing the Destructive Habits. You will understand how to properly identify the problems in your life as well as taking responsibility for their solutions. You will put the elements of InsideOut Empowerment into action so you can become the person you want to be, create the relationships you desire, and live your life with inner peace and happiness.

InsideOut Empowerment **Coaching**
Regardless of how well you learn the principles in this book or the seminar, life can become challenging at times. You don't feel well, you're tired, you're stressed, out of time and before you know it, you revert to the behaviors that you know so well. InsideOut Coaching provides just the right balance of support and challenge to keep you on the road to applying these principles consistently for maximum benefit. Coaching will help you solidify your recent InsideOut behaviors, patterns of thinking and feelings into your new default programming. It is the fastest, most definite path to overcoming self-sabotage and creating new InsideOut habits for life.

InsideOut Empowerment **CD Course (Coming Soon)**

I am creating a CD course—your personal learning program—that you can listen to in your home, office, or on your commute. As you listen, I will lead you step-by-step into developing the habits of InsideOut Empowerment so you can truly take control of your life by becoming the person you want to be and creating the relationships you want.

InsideOut Empowerment **Keynote Presentations**

Allow me to share the life-changing, transformational components of InsideOut Empowerment at your event. These ideas are applicable in self-development, personal relationships, parenting, and workplace relationships—anywhere there are people who would like to improve their relationships with people in their lives, including themselves. People who are satisfied in their relationships are more productive, creative, happy, and satisfied everywhere in their lives.

Become an *InsideOut* **Coach**

Begin the five-step process to become a coach, using the InsideOut Empowerment process. You can add InsideOut Empowerment to your already existing coaching skills, master InsideOut Empowerment and open your own coaching practice, or learn InsideOut coaching to use in your supervision and management of employees or students.

For more information on these and other programs, please visit www.InsideOutEmpowerment.com/programs.php.

Appendix Two

Book Club Discussion Questions

Discussion Guidelines:
Because the material in this book can generate deeply personal discussions, some guidelines for these discussions are suggested. When discussing this book in a group, feel free to use the following guidelines or create some of your own.

1. Anyone at anytime can pass on any question.

2. Use only Healthy Relationship Habits when discussing anything about your current partners.

3. Own the opinions you express; you have every right to them. However, simply state your opinions. Do not attempt to convince others that you are correct. There are no "right" answers.

4. Do not offer advice unless someone specifically requests it. Respect proper boundaries.

Chapter 1

1. How many couples do you know who would have qualified to take Olver's relationship survey?

2. What are your thoughts about the Platinum versus the Golden Rule?

3. Do you believe that one person alone can improve a relationship?

Chapter 2

4. Which of the four relationship stages are you in?

5. What are some things you have done to successfully turn lonely into simply being alone?

6. What do you think about Olver's concept of becoming the person who will attract your soulmate into your life?

Chapter 3

7. Where are some places that singles can go to meet each other?

8. Have you made your list for your soulmate? What traits, qualities, and characteristics have you included? If already in a relationship, what qualities does your partner possess that are on your list?

9. What are some things you do to promote effective communication in your relationship?

Chapter 4

10. Do you have a favorite Destructive Relationship Habit, one you tend to use regularly?

11. Since reading about the Destructive Habits, have you noticed when you use them?

12. If you were to choose one Healthy Habit to implement this week which one would it be, and why?

Chapter 5

13. What is your particular Needs-Strength Profile?

14. What did you think of Olver's discussion of the three ways people can meet their need for power?

15. Do you experience any particular need-strength conflict in your relationship? If so, what can you do to reduce the conflict?

Chapter 6

16. What are your vision, mission, and values?

17. For you, which areas of your life (financial, relational, mental/intellectual, physical and spiritual) need to be most aligned with your life partner?

18. What questions do you think are most important to ask when determining compatibility for a long-term relationship?

Chapter 7

19. Has your relationship followed the pattern of The Seasons of Love? Explain.

20. What are some autumn challenges that have caused stress in your relationship?

21. Under what circumstances might you opt to leave your relationship and return to the Alone Stage?

Chapter 8

22. Where do you and your relationship fall on the Dependence / Interdependence / Independence Continuum?

23. Where would you like to be on the continuum?

24. Have you noticed your position changing over the years? How so?

Chapter 9

25. What do you think about jealousy in a committed relationship?

26. If someone expresses a sexual interest in you, would you tell your partner? Why or why not?

27. What do you think about the concept of having an Upper Limit Problem?

Chapter 10

28. What do you think about the differences between men and women when it comes to sex and romance? Do you think Olver is on target?

29. Which of these differences have you seen contribute to the breakdown of relationships you know?

30. Can you attempt to answer question #29 from the other gender's perspective. If you are a female, can you answer the previous question from a man's perspective? If you are male, can you do the same from a female's perspective?

Chapter 11

31. Can you see yourself in any of the areas Olver discusses in the section on Communication Differences? What are your particular patterns?

32. Do you tend to want love or respect from your partner? What do you offer most to him or her?

33. Do you have Rules of Engagement, whether spoken or not? If so, what are they?

Chapter 12

34. What problem are *you* having that you blame your partner for and expect him or her to fix for you?

35. Do you have any deal breakers?

36. What do you think about the idea that ending a relationship prevents an opportunity for growth?

Chapter 13

37. Of the affairs you have known, would you say that the partner not involved in a sexual relationship with someone else was involved in a more socially-accepted version of an "affair"? Why or why not?

38. Do you think keeping an affair a secret is a valid way for a relationship to survive? Why or why not?

39. Do you think the 3-Step Process for surviving affairs really works?

Chapter 14

40. Have you experienced the serenity that comes from accepting something you don't like about your partner's character or behavior?

41. Have you learned to appreciate a difference about your partner? If so, how did you do it and what changed as a result?

42. Why is appreciating differences so much better than simply accepting them?

Chapter 15

43. What do you think of the idea of a Talking Stick when trying to resolve differences in your relationship?

44. Share an example of a conflict you solved with a win/win/win outcome.

45. How do you think the use of the Solving Circle would work in your relationship?

Chapter 16

46. What are some things you do to maintain your relationship?

47. Of Chapman's *Five Love Languages*, which one do you think is your primary one? How about your partner's?

48. What did you think of Fitzgerald's poem? Did it resonate with you?

Chapter 17

49. What are the things you consciously do to nurture your relationship?

50. What kind of boundaries do you maintain between your relationship and others?

51. Have you experienced others judging or giving advice about your relationship? What did you do?

Chapter 18

52. What do you think about grief serving a purpose? Can you see ways in which grief can meet people's needs?

53. What do you think about the relationship options of leave it, change it, or accept it?

54. Share a time you experienced a relationship ending and were able to see the benefits, even it was only in hindsight.

Appendix Three

The Survey

1. Are you male or female?

2. What is your race?

3. On a 1-5 scale with 5 being the happiest, how happy are you with your relationship?

4. How many years have you been together?

5. Are you married, living together, or committed living separately?

6. How do you define a quality relationship?

7. What are the ingredients that make your relationships work?

8. What are the things you consciously do to nurture your relationship?

9. What are the three things you appreciate most about your partner?

10. What have been your biggest relationship challenges? How did you overcome them?

11. Are you or have you raised children together? (children you have together, step children, adopted children, foster children) How many of each?

12. Have you ever gone to relationship counseling? Yes or No If yes, how many times? For how long? What did you learn or change because of it?

13. Are there any deal breakers that would cause you to end your relationship? (yes or no) If yes, what would they be?

14. Did you ever have a point or points in your relationship when you considered ending it? Yes or No. If yes, explain what was happening and why you decided to stay.

15. Have you had other intimate relationships outside of your primary relationship? If so, how many and how long did they last? Does your partner know? Did this/these affairs help or hurt your relationship? In what way?

16. Is religion/spirituality a prominent part of your life? Yes or No If yes, what is your religion?

17. (On the scale from 1–5 with 5 being most satisfied) How satisfied are you with your partner financially?

18. (On the scale from 1–5 with 5 being most satisfied) How satisfied are you with your partner relationally?

19. (On the scale from 1–5 with 5 being most satisfied) How satisfied are you with your partner mentally and intellectually?

20. (On the scale from 1–5 with 5 being most satisfied) How satisfied are you with your partner physically?

21. (On the scale from 1–5 with 5 being most satisfied) How satisfied are you with your partner spiritually?

22. What are the three most important things you have in common?

23. If you could change up to three things about your partner, what would they be and why?

24. What factors do you believe have contributed to the longevity of your relationship?

25. What are some challenges you faced and how did you work them out?

26. How do you and your partner resolve conflicts in your relationship?

27. If you were giving advice about relationships to a young couple today, what would you say?

28. If you are chosen as one of the 100 couples to be included in my next book, are you willing to be interviewed more extensively either in person or by phone?

Appendix Four

Characteristics and Behaviors of Happy Couples

When asked what ingredients make their relationship work, the couples I surveyed responded:

1. Communication		59%
2. **Respect***		50%
3. **Trust***/Honesty		49%
4. Time Together/Quality Time/Companionship		47%
5. **Support***/**Encouragement***		39%
6. Humor/Laughter		37%
7. Prioritizing the Relationship or One's Partner over Self		34%
8. Commitment/Loyalty		33%
9. **Listening***		31%
10. Great Sex		29%
11. Common Interests		29%
12. **Accepting***		29%
13. Shared Spirituality		25%
14. Similar Beliefs and Values		23%
15. Time Apart/Freedom to be One's Own Person/ Individuality		23%
16. Friendship		23%
17. **Negotiation***/Give & Take		21%
18. Having Fun Together		19%
19. Physical Touch/Affection		19%
20. Understanding/Compassion/Empathy		17%
21. Having Common Goals		15%
22. Expressions of Appreciation or Affirmations/Saying "I Love You"		13%
23. Forgiveness		11%

24. Patience	7%
25. Challenging Partner to be His or Her Best/Holding Accountable	6%
26. Focus on Personal Growth	6%
27. Praying Together	6%
28. Shared Responsibility	6%
29. Giving Gifts	5%
30. Mutual Attraction	5%
31. Financial Compatibility	4%
32. Complimentary Strengths and Weaknesses/Balance	4%
33. Kindness	4%
34. Safety	4%
35. Surprising Each Other	4%
36. Flexibility	3%
37. Interdependence	1%
38. Humility	<1%
39. No Blaming	<1%
40. Sharing Love Rituals	<1%

* Dr. William Glasser's seven Healthy Relationship Habits

Appendix Five

Relationship Resources

Dr. Gary Chapman seeks to fulfill his call to the ministry as a pastor, speaker, and author. He speaks extensively throughout the U.S. and internationally on marriage, family, and relationships. Sales exceeding 5 million copies earned him the Platinum Book Award from the Evangelical Publishers Association for *The Five Love Languages*, which has been translated into over thirty-six languages. Twenty-seven other books and five video series are also among his publications. You can find him at www.garychapman.org.

Dr John Demartini is a human behavioral specialist, founder of the Demartini Institute and a bestselling author and business consultant working with CEOs of fortune 500 companies, celebrities and sports personalities. Dr Demartini's work incorporates a broad spectrum of disciplines and is relevant for any aspect of self development from dealing with emotions to awakening leadership in self and in others. Check him out at www.drdemartini.com.

Arielle Ford has mastered the art of making things happen. A nationally recognized publicist and marketing expert, producer, author and consultant she has catapulted many authors and celebrities to stardom and enormously facilitated the rapid growth of the self-help and human potential movement in the US. Learn more at www.soulmatesecret.com.

Dr. William Glasser is an internationally recognized psychiatrist who is best known as the author of Reality Therapy, a method of psychotherapy he created in 1965 that is now taught all over the world. Glasser's path has been one of a continuing progression from private practice to lecturing and writing and ultimately culminating in the publication of over twenty books. Dr. Glasser teaches that if we can't figure out how to satisfy our power need by respecting each other, our days on earth are numbered. He offers choice theory to replace external control and has dedicated the remainder of his life to teaching and supporting this idea. Although Dr. Glasser is mostly retired, he is still a much sought-after speaker, nationally and internationally. See more about him at www.wglasser.com.

Dr. John Gray is an expert in the field of communication. His focus is to help men and women understand, respect and appreciate their differences in both personal and professional relationships. In his many books, CDs, DVDs, tapes, workshops and seminars, he provides simple, practical tools and insights to effectively manage stress and improve relationships at all stages and ages by creating the brain and body chemistry of health, happiness and lasting romance. Check him out at http://home.marsvenus.com.

Gay Hendricks, Ph.D., has served for more than 35 years as one of the major contributors to the fields of relationship transformation and body-mind therapies. Along with his wife, Dr. Kathlyn Hendricks, Gay is the co-author of many bestsellers, including *Conscious Loving* and *Five Wishes*. Dr. Hendricks received his Ph.D. in counseling psychology from Stanford in 1974. After a twenty-one-year career as a professor of Counseling Psychology at University Colorado, he and Kathlyn founded The Hendricks Institute, which is based in Ojai, California, and offers seminars worldwide. You can find him at www.hendricks.com.

Kathlyn Hendricks, Ph.D., A.D.T.R., has been a pioneer in the field of body-mind integration for nearly forty years. Her explorations about the catalytic transformational power of the creative arts have been featured in many magazines, journals and books. She received her doctorate in transpersonal psychology in 1982 and has been a Board Certified-Dance/Movement Therapist of the American Dance Therapy Association since 1975. You can find her at www.hendricks.com.

Harville Hendrix, Ph.D., is a Clinical Pastoral Counselor who is known internationally for his work with couples. He and his wife Helen LaKelly Hunt, Ph.D. cocreated Imago Relationship Therapy and developed the concept of "conscious partnership." Their partnership and collaboration has resulted in nine books on intimate relationships and parenting. Harville and Helen have six children and live in New York and New Mexico. Check him out at www.harvillehendrix.com.

Karen Kan, MD, Law of Attraction Relationship Author and Coach, coaches single men and women worldwide how to attract their ideal love partner by harnessing the Law of Attraction through her blogs, newsletters, radio shows and privately. Her step-by-step e-Book, *Creating Your Fairytale Love Life*, teaches you the seven steps to manifesting your dream partner based on her own personal experience and professional training with various spiritual teachers. Sign up for her *Attracting Love e-Course* available FREE at www.LawofAttractioninLove.com.

Paul and Layne Cutright are relationship and communication experts, bestselling authors, speakers, trainers and evolutionary relationship coaches. Professionals in the field of human potential since 1976, they share a dynamic romantic, creative and professional partnership that has taken them all over the world. Layne and Paul offer a practical, skill-based, systems approach to relationships education and coaching that includes four progressive tracks; 1. authentic, heart-centered communication; 2. enlightened conflict resolution; 3. emotional healing and well-being; and 4. creative laws of relationships for consciously creating relationships of all kinds. Paul and Layne can be found on the web at HYPERLINK "http://www.PaulandLayne.com" www.PaulandLayne.com where you may learn more about their programs.

Dr. Kevin Leman, an internationally renowned psychologist and bestselling author of more than 30 books, provides easy techniques, helpful tips and clear insight that will change the way you look at and resolve the parenting, marriage and relationship issues in your life. He brings common sense to common problems. Dealing with topics that range from raising children and birth order to business and marriage, Dr. Leman tells it like it is. With just the right touch of humor, his parenting books, couples advice and perspective on family and relationships deliver real-life answers to real-life problems. Find him at www.drleman.com.

Marci Shimoff is the woman's face of the biggest self-help book phenomenon in history, *Chicken Soup for the Soul*. Marci is one of the bestselling female nonfiction authors of all time. In addition, she's a featured teacher in the international film and book phenomenon, *The Secret*. Her new book, *HAPPY FOR NO REASON: 7 Steps to Being Happy from the Inside Out*, offers a revolutionary approach to experiencing deep and lasting happiness.

A celebrated transformational leader and one of the nation's leading experts on happiness, success, and the law of attraction, Marci has inspired millions of people around the world, sharing her breakthrough methods for personal fulfillment and professional success. Check out her website at www.happyfornoreason.com.

Eckhart Tolle's profound yet simple teachings have already helped countless people throughout the world find inner peace and greater fulfillment in their lives. At the core of the teachings lies the transformation of consciousness, a spiritual awakening that he sees as the next step in human evolution. An essential aspect of this awakening consists in transcending our ego-based state of consciousness. This is a prerequisite not only for personal happiness but also for the ending of violent conflict endemic on our planet. Find him at www.eckharttolle.com.

Nancy S. Buck, Ph.D., completed her doctoral studies in developmental psychology with a specialization in parenting. She has created Peaceful Parenting® applying choice theory to parenting. This represents not only her twenty years of studying and teaching choice theory around the country but also her twenty years of parenting her identical twin sons. Nancy's genuine, warm and authentic teaching style is clear and concise, helping learners move from the theoretical to the practical. Because the theory is clearly and continuously explained and referred to, learners not only understand HOW to parent more effectively, they also understand WHY moving from external control parenting to internal control parenting is more effective.

Sandra Haynes works as a counsellor in private practice in the southern suburbs of Adelaide, and is a professional member of the Counselling Association of South Australia. While she works with individuals as well as couples, the focus of her ongoing professional development is in relationship counselling. She believes people are the experts in their own life with the potential to grow and change as well as to resolve their own problems. Check out her website at www.sandrahaynescounselling.com.au.

John Wilder, a marriage, relationship and sexual coach, is one of but a handful of clinicians who treat clients holistically, dealing with all 3 aspects of our being; mind, body and spirit. He helps people stop fighting with their spouses and peacefully resolve their differences. John also helps spouses improve their sexual relationship with more and better sex. You can follow his blog for marriage, relationship or sexual issues at marriage-coach.wordpress.com. Just leave him a comment on his blog or email him at marriagecoach1@yahoo.com. He even offers a money-back guarantee.

Coach Steve Toth has more then twenty years experience in life coaching, leadership development, management consulting, professional coaching and culture change. He has worked with hundreds of executives, entrepreneurs and professionals as a personal-executive coach. He studied at the Management Consulting Institute, Context Training, Landmark Education, PAIRS Foundation, Transformational Breath Institute, and Naropa University. He founded Real Coaching Institute to provide coaching programs and consulting services that dramatically enhance individual and team performance in the areas of Sales, Motivation, Leadership, Teamwork, Communication and Life Balance Management Skills.

Sarah Elizabeth Malinak, M.Div. and her husband, Joseph Malinak, are the authors of *Getting Back to Love: When the Pushing and Pulling Threaten to Tear You Apart,* the definitive book on the romantic challenges facing adult mama's boys and daddy's girls. The owners of Creating Ideal Relationships, LLC, Sarah and Joseph are Relationship Coaches and mentors residing in Asheville, NC. Visit them at IdealRelationships.com.

Melody Glatz Founder of SinglesDatingConvention.com, is an Entrepreneur, Dating and Relationship Expert, Lover of Life, Critique Queen and now fondly called the go-to-girl of dating/the new "Hitch-ette." She provides insight in the wonderful world of what she loves and doesn't love—without restriction on her website, MelodyLovesThis.com. Her philosophy is that we're each gifted with many talents and a unique voice—hers happens to be quirky, colorful, energetic and honest. She'll make you laugh, make you cry and engage you in lively conversations. She believes that we're all here to help each other gain in knowledge, wisdom and understanding about life. You can also find her on Twitter on both @melodylovesthis and @singlesevent.

Sarah Michaels is a down-to-earth, real-life woman with a mission to help other women find the happiness, security and love they desire and deserve. Visit Sarah at www.youcangettheguy.com for down to earth advice on love, relationships, attraction and more.

Dr. Dennis Neder is a renowned dating, sex and relationship expert and the best-selling author of the series, "Being a Man in a Woman's World." He is also a talk show host and has appeared on over 2500 TV and radio shows as expert, guest and host. To learn more about Dr. Dennis and his work, please visit: www.BeingAMan.com.

Marcus "Dr. Respect" Gentry is the president of Marcus Gentry & Associates, a company that develops and delivers programs that enhance personal and professional growth; build habits of success; improve performance; and increase awareness. As a spiritual adviser, coach, consultant and public speaker, Dr. Respect has challenged his clients and audiences to live their best life for the past 25 years. He is author of *101 Ponderables* and the forthcoming book, *101 Ponderables: If You Dare,* a provocative set of questions designed to engage groups in deeper levels of conversation. For more information visit www.marcusgentry.com.

Don Childers has 28 years experience counseling people with relationship issues; couples with family and marital problems; parents needing help with teens; and with gay/lesbian couples wanting a healthier relationship. Improving relationships is his specialty. Don is Reality Therapy Certified since 1992. He focuses on the present, not the past. Don focuses on solutions, not the problem or symptoms. Check out his website at www.childerscounseling.com.

Ken Donaldson is a licensed mental health counselor; board certified as an addictions professional and clinical hypnotherapist; and certified as a master relationship coach. Ken is the author of *Marry YourSelf First! Say "I Do" to a Life of Passion, Power, Purpose and Prosperity* (www.MarryYourSelfFirstBook.com). Ken's mission is to help professionals and their families eliminate stress, maximize success and create extraordinary relationships at home, at work and in the community. He comes off the stage and into the hearts and minds of all participants who attend his presentations. Visit Ken's website at http://KenDonaldson.com.

Patricia A. Robey, Ed.D, LPC, NCC, CTRTC, is an assistant professor of counseling at Governors State University, University Park, Illinois. She is a licensed professional counselor and specializes in applying reality therapy and choice theory in her work with individuals, couples, families and groups. Dr. Robey is a senior faculty member of the William Glasser Institute and has taught the concepts of Choice Theory and Reality Therapy in the United States and internationally.

Beth Banning and Neill Gibson believe that the shortest path to a happy life is found through conscious choice. Their mission is to play a significant role in supporting the global evolution toward greater consciousness. They are confident that the most effective way for this shift to happen is one relationship at a time, beginning with the relationship we have with ourselves. Learn more at FocusedAttention.com and NewAgeSelfHelp.com.

Rodney and Karen Grubbs, ecstatically happily married for over 30 years, authors and speakers, are founders of NeverEndingHoneymoon.com and creators of the "52 Weekly Marriage Boosters" series, weekly email tips and strategies to keep that Never Ending Honeymoon marriage alive and thriving. Sign up for free at www.MyMarriageBoosters.com. Their upcoming book, *The Perfect First Year,* will bless your life with actionable tips and strategies to build your marriage into a Never Ending Honeymoon.

Poon Meng Seng retired from the education service in Singapore in 1996, having headed and taught in secondary schools for some thirty years. He attended a three month course at the Institute of Holy Land Studies in Jerusalem upon retirement. As an ordained Elder of the Presbyterian Church, he has been active in Christian Education, and the training of church planters and trainers for the Developing World. He now spends time developing materials for their needs.

Lissa Coffey is a lifestyle and relationship expert, media personality, and the founder of CoffeyTalk.com. Her new book is "CLOSURE and the Law of Relationship: Endings as New Beginnings." Deepak Chopra says: "Highly recommended!" More information at: www.closurebook.com.

SpiritualSingles.com is the largest, exclusively conscious dating site on the Internet with thousands of single members available and ready to create a committed, loving, spiritual partnership. This is a great resource to meet someone who values spiritual growth, living a holistic, healthy life, meditation, yoga, world peace and being environmentally conscious. www.SpiritualSingles.com

Sylvester Baugh is Director of Baugh Training and Consulting in Illinois. He provides training, consultation, and coaching for individuals, agencies, and other institutions. For over 20 years Sylvester served as the Training Manager for a multi-faceted family service center in Park Forest, Ilinois, where he trained and consulted with teachers, social workers, other business professionals, and at-risk-youth. Sylvester provides trainings and workshops in the areas of Cultural Awareness, Managing Conflict, Team Building, Leadership, and much more.

Ligia Houben is an inspirational speaker and educator in the area of life transitions. Her work has been centered in the area of grief and loss, expanding into meaning and growth. She is a life coach, consultant and grief counselor and has delivered her message from corporations to hospitals. Ligia has appeared in numerous radio and TV shows, including CNN Español, NBC, and NPR. She is the author of the self-help book *Transform your Loss: An Anthology of Strength and Hope,* which contains "The Eleven Principles of Transformation,™" a system that involves the emotional, spiritual, and cognitive aspects of the person as they face a transition or loss. Ligia created this system of transformation to help people transform their losses and change their lives.

Krisanna Jeffery is a Registered Clinical Counsellor and Sex Educator trained at the University of Victoria and the Institute for Advanced Study of Human Sexuality. She has had the privilege to work on issues of relationships and sexuality with many couples and individuals as a practicing psychotherapist since 1983, on Vancouver Island, British Columbia. Krisanna has dedicated her life to helping others be the best they can be! In 2007 she published *The Great Sex for Life Toolkit,* a book, CD, and DVD package to help people appreciate and expand their understanding of their sexuality. She currently does public speaking on the topic of healthy sexuality and coaches couples in person and by phone.

Love Coach Rinatta helps singles attract lasting love and helps couples rediscover their love for each other. She is an internationally known love coach, dating, relationship and marriage expert, and author of numerous published articles and e-books on how to attract and keep a great relationship or marriage. Visit her website www.LoveCoachForYou.com or find her on facebook at www.Facebook.com/LoveCoachRinatta.

Neil Ward is one of the UK's top dating coaches. Having started the transition to becoming a dating coach at age 20, he now has years of experience and is widely respected with great credibility throughout thousands of people worldwide. His method is somewhat unique; he doesn't teach any special tricks, tactics, chat up lines or to fake it until you make it. His philosophy is to take you as you are and develop you into an amazing person that naturally attracts people into your life. Regardless of your barriers towards dating, Neil will help you to smash through any limiting beliefs you have and to come out into the light a leader in the dating game.

Margaret Paul, Ph.D. is a best-selling author/co-author of 8 books, including the best-selling *Do I Have To Give Up Me To Be Loved By You?*

She is a relationship expert, and co-creator of the powerful Inner Bonding® process—and of the popular website, www.innerbonding.com.

Betsy Sansby, MS, Licensed Marriage and Family Therapist. She is the creator of The OuchKit, LoveBites, and other communication tools for couples. She is also the author of Ask Betsy, an online relationship advice column, which you can read at TalkAboutRelationships.net. She has appeared in *Redbook Magazine*, and is regularly featured therapist in the popular *Ladies' Home Journal* series *"Can This Marriage Be Saved?"*

Dana Vince is a Licensed Counselor in the Tampa area of Florida. She specializes in working with couples and families and is married with 2 children of her own. You can check out her website at www.healingheartscounseling.org/about-dana.

Index

About Kim Olver

Kim Olver is an internationally acclaimed transformational leader. She has inspired thousands of people around the globe to apply the principles of InsideOut Empowerment.

In 1987, Kim began her spiritual journey by taking a Basic Intensive Training in Reality Therapy with Dr. Nancy Buck, a certified William Glasser Institute Instructor. Dr. Buck inspired her to follow a similar path. In 1992, Kim became certified in Reality Therapy and in 1993, she also became an approved instructor for the William Glasser Institute. As such, over the years she has trained thousands in reality therapy and Choice Theory®.

Since that time, she has developed her own process called Inside-Out Empowerment. Naturally, this process has its roots in Dr. Glasser's foundational teachings and goes beyond reality therapy to delve into the subconscious sabotage we often engage in as we near reaching our deepest dreams.

Kim got her counseling degree at the University of Scranton in 1996 and is a licensed clinical professional counselor, as well as a nationally certified counselor. She worked over 20 years in the field of social service, the majority of that time spent working with specialized foster children and their families.

In 1999, Kim's husband of 16 years died of leukemia, leaving her with two teenage boys to raise. This was a pivotal point in her life. She decided to take the principles she had been teaching and fully apply them to her own life to help manage the grief and to become an effective single parent.

In 2004, Kim moved to Chicago and began her own coaching, training and consulting business and founded the InsideOut Empowerment Institute, whose mission is to help people get along better with the important people in their lives, including themselves, at home and at work. She works with couples, parents, individuals seeking self-growth, and businesses who understand the importance of quality relationships.

When our important relationships are functioning smoothly, then other things seem to almost take care of themselves. Kim's first book, *Leveraging Diversity at Work*, was written to help people understand any problems people have connecting and understanding each other begin within oneself.

InsideOut Empowerment stresses two major concepts: 1) The only person's behavior you can control is your own and 2) Whenever you are experiencing conflict or struggle, the best place to find the solution is through changing something you can control—either your thoughts or actions.

This book, *Secrets of Happy Couples,* was written to help people in committed relationships find happiness within themselves and with each other. It is the second in the InsideOut Empowerment Series.

To find out more about Kim's keynote presentations, books, or seminar programs, you can contact her at:

Coaching for Excellence LLC
PO Box 2666
Country Club Hills, IL 60478
Phone: 708-957-6047
Fax: 708-957-8028
www.kimolver.com
www.secretsofhappycouples.com

Quick Order Form

Fax Orders: 570-729-1543. Send this form.
Telephone orders: Call 570-729-1543. Have your credit card ready.
Email orders: orders@insideoutpress.com
Online orders: http://www.kimolver.com/webstore_books.php
Postal Orders: Inside Out Press, P.O. Box 2666,
                     Country Club Hills, IL 60478

Please send the following books. I understand that I may return any of them for a full refund.

_____

_____

_____

_____

Please send more FREE information on:
__ Other Books __ Speaking/Seminars __ Coaching/Consulting
__ Publishing

Name: _____

Address: _____

City: _____ State: _____ Zip: _____

Telephone: _____

Email address: _____

Sales Tax: Please add 9.75% for products shipped to Illinois.
Shipping:
U.S.: Priority Mail: $5.45 for first book and $1.00 for each additional
                   book.
      Media Mail: $2.88 for first book and $.75 for each additional book.
International: $13.45 for first book; $9.00 for each additional book
                   (estimate).